Dona Orr
Boise State University
Boise, Idaho

Carol W. Henson
Clayton State College
Morrow, Georgia

H. Frances Daniels
East Carolina University
Greenville, North Carolina

Australia • Canada • Mexico • Singapore • Spain • United Kingdom • United States

Instructor's Manual for
The Basics of Proofreading: A Programmed Approach, 4th Edition
By Dona Orr, Carol W. Henson, and H. Frances Daniels

Editor-in-Chief
Jack Calhoun

Vice President/Executive Publisher
Dave Shaut

Team Leader
Karen Schmohe

Acquisitions Editor
Joseph Vocca

Production Manager
Tricia Matthews Boies

Production Editor
Tim Bailey

Consulting Editor
Marianne Miller

Contributing Writer
Julie Roehl Coffin
Educational Consultant
Columbus, Ohio

Executive Marketing Manager
Carol Volz

Channel Manager
Chris McNamee

Marketing Coordinator
Lori Pegg

Art and Design Coordinator
Tippy McIntosh

Manufacturing Coordinator
Kevin Kluck

Editorial Assistant
Stephanie L. White

Production Assistant
Nancy Stamper

Cover Design
Lou Ann Thesing

Compositor
Lachina Publishing Services,
Cleveland, Ohio

Printer
Courier Corporation,
Kendallville, Indiana

Electronic Media
Limited Warranty

South-Western Educational Publishing ("South-Western") extends the following warranty to only the original customer:

Warranty Coverage
This warranty covers the media on which the South-Western software/data are recorded. This limited warranty does not extend to the information contained on the media and in the accompanying book materials (the "Software/data"). The media product is warranted against malfunction due to defective materials or construction. This warranty is void if the media product is damaged by accident or unreasonable use, neglect, installation, improper service, or other causes not arising out of defects in material or construction.

Warranty Duration
The media product is warranted for a period of three months from the date of the original purchase by the customer.

Warranty Disclaimers
The following should be read and understood before purchasing and/or using the media:

a. Any implied warranties that arise out of this sale are limited in duration to the above three-month period. South-Western will not be liable for loss of use of the media or other incidental or consequential costs, expenses, or damages incurred by you, the consumer, or any other user. Furthermore, South-Western will not be liable for any claim of any kind whatsoever by any other party against the user of the Software/data.

b. South-Western does not warrant that the Software/data and the media will be free from error or will meet the specific requirements of the consumer. You, the consumer, assume complete responsibility for any decisions made or actions taken based on information obtained using the Software/data.

c. Any statements made concerning the utility of the Software/data are not to be construed as expressed or implied warranties.

d. SOUTH-WESTERN MAKES NO WARRANTY, EITHER EXPRESSED OR IMPLIED, INCLUDING BUT NOT LIMITED TO ANY IMPLIED WARRANTY OR MERCHANTABILITY AND FITNESS FOR A PARTICULAR PURPOSE, REGARDING THE SOFT-WARE/DATA AND MAKES ALL SOFTWARE/ DATA AVAILABLE SOLELY ON AN "AS IS" BASIS.

e. In no event will South-Western be liable to anyone for special collateral, incidental, or consequential damages in connection with or arising out of the purchase or use of the Software/data. The sole and exclusive liability of South-Western, regardless of the form of action, will not exceed the purchase price of the media.

f. Some states do not allow the exclusion or limitation of implied warranties or consequential damages, so the above limitations or exclusions may not apply to you in those states.

Further Disclaimers of Warranty
South-Western will extend no warranty where the software is used on a machine other than that designated on the software package.

Media Replacement
Provided that you, the customer, have satisfactorily completed and returned a copy of the License Agreement, South-Western will replace, during the warranty period, any defective media at no charge. At South-Western's option, the defective media must be returned, postage prepaid, along with proof of purchase date. Please contact South-Western at the address shown below for return instructions before returning any defective media.

South-Western Educational Publishing
Media Services
5191 Natorp Boulevard
Mason, OH 45040

Legal Remedies
This warranty gives you specific legal rights, and you may also have other rights that vary from state to state.

Technical Support Hotline

The Technical Support Hotline is available by phone, fax, or e-mail from 8:30 a.m.–6:00 p.m. EST to help you with any technical problems you may be having with this media product.

Phone: 1-800-423-0563
Fax: 859-647-5045
E-mail: support@kdc.com (24-hour response)

If you identify a problem, please check your hardware to make sure it is working properly. If the hardware is functioning correctly, call the number given. Please have the following information and materials with you when calling the hotline:

- Program or template CD-ROM
- Text
- Instructor's manual
- List of any error messages
- Students' printouts
- Description of the problem
- Computer type and model
- Computer's memory configuration
- Version number of operating system
- Name and version number of commercial software (if applicable)

Please do not permit your students access to the hotline contact information. If you want to order software, call Thomson Learning at (800) 354-9706.

CONTENTS

INTRODUCTION   vii
    Icons   vii
    Supplementary Technology Resource   vii
    Design of the Instructor's Manual   viii
    Design of the Course   viii
    Master Chart of Chapter Content,
        Checkpoints, and Applications   x

GENERAL TEACHING SUGGESTIONS   xiv
    Tips for Student Success   xiv
    Student Learning Styles   xv
    Cooperative Learning   xv
    Use of Examples and Nonexamples   xvi
    Student Evaluation   xvi

CHAPTER 1   **Proofreading for Quality Control**   1
    Classroom Strategies and Learning Activities   1
    Computerized Proofreading Activities   1

CHAPTER 2   **Keyboarding Errors**   2
    Transparency Masters   2
    Classroom Strategies and Learning Activities   2
    Computerized Proofreading Activities   3

CHAPTER 3   **Abbreviation Errors**   4
    Transparency Masters   4
    Classroom Strategies and Learning Activities   4
    Computerized Proofreading Activities   5

CHAPTER 4   **Word Division Errors**   5
    Transparency Masters   5
    Classroom Strategies and Learning Activities   6
    Computerized Proofreading Activities   7

CHAPTER 5   **Number Expression Errors**   7
    Transparency Masters   7
    Classroom Strategies and Learning Activities   7
    Computerized Proofreading Activities   8

CHAPTER 6   **Format Errors**   9
    Transparency Masters   9
    Classroom Strategies and Learning Activities   9
    Computerized Proofreading Activities   11

CHAPTER 7   **Grammar Errors: Sentence Structure**   11
    Transparency Masters   11
    Classroom Strategies and Learning Activities   12
    Computerized Proofreading Activities   13

CHAPTER 8   **Grammar Errors: Pronoun Agreement and Selection**   13
Transparency Masters   13
Classroom Strategies and Learning Activities   13
Computerized Proofreading Activities   15

CHAPTER 9   **Errors in Words Often Confused**   15
Transparency Masters   15
Classroom Strategies and Learning Activities   15
Computerized Proofreading Activities   17

CHAPTER 10   **Punctuation Errors, Part 1**   17
Transparency Masters   17
Classroom Strategies and Learning Activities   17
Computerized Proofreading Activities   19

CHAPTER 11   **Punctuation Errors, Part 2**   19
Transparency Masters   19
Classroom Strategies and Learning Activities   19
Computerized Proofreading Activities   21

CHAPTER 12   **Capitalization Errors**   22
Transparency Masters   22
Classroom Strategies and Learning Activities   22
Computerized Proofreading Activities   23

CHAPTER 13   **Editing for Content**   23
Transparency Masters   23
Classroom Strategies and Learning Activities   24
Computerized Proofreading Activities   25

CHAPTER 14   **Editing For Conciseness**   25
Transparency Masters   25
Classroom Strategies and Learning Activities   25
Computerized Proofreading Activities   26

CHAPTER 15   **Editing for Clarity**   27
Transparency Masters   27
Classroom Strategies and Learning Activities   27
Computerized Proofreading Activities   28

TEMPLATE CD ACTIVITIES AND SOLUTIONS   29

TRANSPARENCY MASTERS   55

CHAPTER QUIZZES/TESTS AND SOLUTIONS   121
Pretest   123
Quizzes   127
Posttest   157

INTRODUCTION

The Basics of Proofreading: A Programmed Approach teaches proofreading and editing concepts and presents drill applications for students to use in gaining skill. For best results, students should complete a business English course before studying *The Basics of Proofreading*. Work connections appear throughout the text and relate directly to the essential basic skills identified through the *Secretary's Commission on Achieving Necessary Skills*, referred to as the SCANS report.[1]

This text may be used as a standalone resource or in conjunction with the entire Basics series. The other texts in the series include *The Basics of English*, *The Basics of Writing*, *The Basics of Speech Communication*, *The Basics of Business Communication*, and *The Basics of Employment Communication*.

The Basics of Proofreading has been revised to expand coverage of selected topics while retaining the format and application focus of the previous edition. The following features support those goals:

- A focus on applying proofreading and editing concepts to written material

- A simple, straight-forward presentation of concepts

- A format that offers instructional flexibility (text may be used for individualized instruction or in a classroom setting)

- Specific learning objectives for each chapter

- Reinforcement of learning through margin notes, workplace connections, cartoons, bloopers, anecdotes, quotations, examples, and chapter summaries

- Checkpoints that challenge students to apply the concepts presented

- End-of-chapter applications, including computerized proofreading applications, that cover major learning objectives

- Solutions for Checkpoints and applications included in the student text

[1]*What Work Requires of Schools: A SCANS Report for America 2000* is a publication of the U.S. Department of Labor, Secretary's Commission on Achieving Necessary Skills, 1991. The Commission spent a year talking with employers, supervisors, and workers to examine changes taking place in the world of work. Their report identified five major competencies and three foundation skill areas required for job performance. Competencies covered the use of resources, interpersonal skills, information, systems, and technology. The foundation for developing these competencies requires development of basic skills, thinking skills, and personal qualities.

The Appendix provides the following reference materials:

- Frequently Misspelled Words
- Two-Letter State Abbreviations
- Common Prepositions

The Instructor's Manual provides these additional features:

- Solutions for optional computerized proofreading applications
- Masters for a pretest, a posttest, and 14 chapter tests (no chapter test is provided for Chapter 1)
- Masters for visuals to be used as transparencies or converted to PowerPoint slides

Icons

The Basics of Proofreading uses icons to identify some of its special features.

Chart of Icons

Icon	Explanation
	The workplace connection icon identifies information that allows students to practice the foundation skills and personal qualities employers look for when hiring.
	The team icon identifies opportunities to work with others and sharpen teamwork skills.
	The Internet icon marks activities where students may practice their online computer skills.
words@work	The *words@work* icon alerts you to specific lessons and exercises from the *words@work* CD-ROM (see Supplemental Technology Resource section below) that correlate with the skills students are developing in each chapter.

Supplementary Technology Resource

South-Western Educational and Professional Publishing offers a supplemental technology resource that supports the learning objectives of *The Basics of Proofreading.*

words@work. Available on CD-ROM, *words@work* provides a self-directed, interactive multimedia environment in which students supplement and reaffirm the material of the course. Following the chapter summaries in *The Basics of Proofreading*, students will notice the ***words@work*** icon and directions to the appropriate activities. Ask your South-Western representative how to obtain ***words@work***.

Design of the Instructor's Manual

The design of the Instructor's Manual assists you in locating desired information quickly and easily. The Instructor's Manual includes the following sections:

Table of Contents. The Table of Contents shows the organization and content of the Instructor's Manual.

The Introduction. The beginning of the Instructor's Manual lists the major features of the student text and provides a master chart of Checkpoints and end-of-chapter applications.

General Teaching Suggestions. The section on General Teaching Suggestions recommends ways to adapt instruction to meet a variety of learning styles and describes teaching strategies.

Chapter Teaching Suggestions. A separate section in this manual covers learning objectives, classroom strategies, additional learning activities, and background on the computerized proofreading applications for each chapter of the student text.

Template CD Applications and Solutions. This section includes the handouts for optional proofreading applications that appear on the template CD-ROM.

Transparency Masters. Instructors may copy and use as transparencies or handouts the transparency masters provided for each chapter. Instructors who use computer projection equipment will find the content from these visuals may easily be adapted for PowerPoint slides.

Chapter Quizzes/Tests and Solutions. The final section of the manual includes quizzes and solutions for each chapter of the student text in addition to a pretest and posttest and solutions.

Design of the Course

The material in this text can be used in a traditional classroom setting, for one-on-one tutoring, or for individualized instruction. Following is a brief summary of the content of each chapter:

Chapter 1   "Proofreading for Quality Control" introduces the concept of proofreading and the language of proofreading symbols. Chapter 1 instructs students in the three-step process of proofreading that is used throughout the text.

Chapter 2   "Keyboarding Errors" alerts students to typical keyboarding errors that appear in written documents. These errors include omissions, additions, misstrokes, and transposition errors, as well as errors that occur in figures, enumerations, and dates.

Chapter 3   "Abbreviation Errors" gives students practice in identifying and correcting errors that occur with abbreviations. Students learn to apply rules of abbreviation.

Chapter 4   "Word Division Errors" covers the rules of word division, including when word division is appropriate and how to properly divide words.

Chapter 5   "Number Expression Errors" presents the rules of style. Students learn when to use either the word style or the figure style for numbers in written text.

Chapter 6   "Format Errors" teaches the correct formats for written business communications that include letters, memoranda, e-mails, and reports. Students apply formatting rules to each of these types of documents.

Chapter 7   "Grammar Errors: Sentence Structure" is the first of two chapters on grammar errors. Students focus on the parts of a complete sentence and on subject/verb agreement. They also learn to identify and correct sentences faults—fragments, comma splices, and run-ons.

Chapter 8   "Grammar Errors: Pronoun Agreement and Selection" is the second of two chapters on grammar errors. Students learn to use proper pronoun case and how to make pronouns agree with antecedents. In addition, students learn to edit for proper pronouns in the use of gender-neutral language.

Chapter 9   "Errors in Words Often Confused" presents words commonly used in business that are often confused because their pronunciation or spelling is similar. The chapter presents 27 sets of words that are often confused plus an additional section of words that are often used incorrectly.

Chapter 10   "Punctuation Errors, Part 1" is the first of two chapters on punctuation errors. This first chapter presents terminal punctuation marks as well as the comma. Students focus on using the comma to separate words and sentence parts.

Chapter 11   "Punctuation Errors, Part 2" is the second of two chapters on punctuation errors. This chapter presents semicolons, colons, apostrophes, quotation marks, underscores, dashes, parentheses, and brackets.

Chapter 12   "Capitalization Errors" gives students practice in applying capitalization rules within text.

Chapter 13   "Editing for Content" is the first of three chapters dealing with editing. Students learn to edit for incorrect facts, inconsistencies, and missing information.

Chapter 14   "Editing for Conciseness" is the second of three chapters dealing with editing. This chapter focuses on errors caused by clichés, imprecise words, and obsolete and redundant expressions. Students learn to identify passive voice and to determine when passive voice is appropriate and how to edit to create active voice when appropriate.

Chapter 15   "Editing for Clarity" is the last of three chapters dealing with editing. Topics covered include errors caused by misplaced and dangling modifiers and lack of parallel construction. Word choice is presented to teach students to choose simple rather than less familiar words and strong verbs rather than noun phrases.

The Basics of Proofreading can be adapted to fit courses ranging from a few weeks to an academic semester. Course length will determine how much time is spent introducing and practicing the proofreading and editing techniques included in each chapter. The following chart suggests the approximate number of days that might be devoted to each chapter in three different time frames.

	6 Weeks (18 class hours)	12 Weeks (36 class hours)	15 Weeks (45 class hours)
Chapters	1+ class hour	2+ class hours	2.5 class hours

MASTER CHART OF CHAPTER CONTENT, CHECKPOINTS, AND APPLICATIONS

Chapter	Checkpoints	Applications
1. Proofreading for Quality Control	NA	NA
2. Keyboarding Errors	2-1 Indicate errors of omission 2-2 Indicate errors of omission and addition 2-3 Indicate errors of omission and addition 2-4 Indicate errors of misstroke 2-5 Indicate errors in a printed list 2-6 Indicate errors in a paragraph 2-7 Indicate transposition errors 2-8 Answer the question 2-9 Spelling Applications	P-1—P-3 Indicate keyboarding and spelling errors Job 1 Indicate errors of omission, addition, and misstroke Job 2 Proofread a purchase order Job 3 Proofread file cards Computerized Proofreading, Job 4 Proofread and edit a page from an employee manual *Computerized Proofreading, Job 5 Proofread and edit a brochure

*Optional template CD activities appear in the Instructor's Manual beginning on page 29.

Introduction

Chapter	Checkpoints	Applications
3. Abbreviation Errors	3-1, 3-2 Indicate abbreviation errors 3-3 Indicate abbreviation errors 3-4, 3-5 Indicate abbreviation errors 3-6—3-8 Indicate abbreviation errors 3-10 Spelling Applications	P-1—P-3 Indicate spelling and abbreviation errors Job 1 Proofread an announcement Job 2 Proofread a customer list Job 3 Proofread an announcement against a rough draft Computerized Proofreading, Job 4 Proofread and format an interoffice memorandum *Computerized Proofreading, Job 5 Proofread and edit an electronic letter of inquiry
4. Word Division Errors	4-1 Indicate correct word division 4-2 Indicate preferred word division 4-3 Indicate preferred word division 4-4 Indicate preferred word division 4-5 Indicate preferred word division 4-6 Indicate preferred word division 4-7 Indicate preferred word division 4-14 Spelling Applications	P-1—P-3 Indicate word division errors Job 1 Proofread form paragraphs Job 2 Proofread a letter Job 3 Proofread a news release Job 4 Proofread a letter against a rough draft Computerized Proofreading, Job 5 Proofread and format a business letter *Computerized Proofreading, Job 6 Proofread and edit a charity auction list
5. Number Expression Errors	5-1—5-5 Indicate errors in the expression of numbers 5-6—5-10 Indicate errors in the expression of numbers 5-11—5-15 Indicate errors in the expression of numbers 5-16—5-20 Indicate errors in the expression of numbers 5-24 Spelling Applications	P-1—P-3 Indicate errors in the expression of numbers and spelling Job 1 Proofread a letter Job 2 Proofread an ad Job 3 Proofread a letter Job 4 Proofread minutes Computerized Proofreading, Job 5 Proofread and format a journal article *Computerized Proofreading, Job 6 Proofread an e-mail message
6. Format Errors	6-1 Answer the question 6-2 Indicate format errors 6-3 Indicate errors in letter style 6-4 Indicate the best letter placement 6-5 Indicate format errors 6-6 Spelling Applications	P-1—P-4 Identify parts of letters P-5 Internet activity Job 1 Proofread a letter Job 2 Proofread a letter Job 3 Proofread a report Job 4 Proofread a letter Computerized Proofreading, Job 5 Format and proofread a memo *Computerized Proofreading, Job 6 Proofread a business letter
7. Grammar Errors: Sentence Structure	7-1, 7-2 Indicate subjects, verbs, and complements 7-3—7-5 Indicate errors in subject-verb agreement 7-6—7-8 Indicate errors in subject-verb agreement 7-9—7-11 Indicate errors in subject-verb agreement 7-12 Indicate errors in subject-verb agreement 7-13 Identify fragments, comma splices, and run-on sentences 7-14 Spelling Applications	P-1—P-4 Indicate grammar and spelling errors P-5 Internet activity Job 1 Proofread a welcome statement Job 2 Proofread an e-mail message Job 3 Proofread a letter Computerized Proofreading, Job 4 Proofread a business letter *Computerized Proofreading, Job 5 Proofread a memo

*Optional template CD activities appear in the Instructor's Manual beginning on page 29.

Chapter	Checkpoints	Applications
8. Grammar Errors: Pronoun Agreement and Selection	8-1 Indicate errors in pronoun selection 8-2 Indicate errors in pronoun selection 8-3 Indicate errors in pronoun selection 8-4 Indicate errors in pronoun selection 8-5—8-7 Indicate errors in pronoun selection 8-8 Indicate errors in pronoun selection 8-9 Spelling Applications	P-1—P-3 Indicate grammar and spelling errors Job 1 Proofread a letter Job 2 Proofread a memo Job 3 Proofread a memo Computerized Proofreading, Job 4 Edit an e-mail message *Computerized Proofreading, Job 5 Proofread a personal business letter
9. Errors in Words Often Confused	9-1 Use of *a, an, of* 9-2 Use of *accept, except* 9-3 Use of *advice, advise* 9-4 Use of *adverse, averse* 9-5 Use of *affect, effect* 9-6 Use of *already, all ready, altogether, all together, always, all ways* 9-7 Use of *anxious, eager* 9-8 Use of *assure, ensure, insure* 9-9 Use of *bad, badly* 9-10 Use of *between, among* 9-11 Use of *bring, take* 9-12 Use of *can/could, may/might* 9-13 Use of *cite, sight, site* 9-14 Use of *complement, compliment* 9-15 Use of *council, counsel* 9-16 Use of *every day, everyday* 9-17 Use of *fewer, less* 9-18 Use of *good, well* 9-19 Use of *imply, infer* 9-20 Use of *lay, lie* 9-21 Use of *loose, lose* 9-22 Use of *passed, past* 9-23 Use of *precede, proceed* 9-24 Use of *principal, principle* 9-25 Use of *stationary, stationery* 9-26 Use of *that, which, who* 9-27 Use of *to, too, two* 9-29 Spelling Applications	P-1—P-4 Indicate errors in word usage and spelling P-5 Internet activity Job 1 Proofread an e-mail message Job 2 Proofread a letter Job 3 Proofread a memo Computerized Proofreading, Job 4 Proofread a memo with a table *Computerized Proofreading, Job 5 Proofread advertising copy
10. Punctuation Errors, Part 1	10-1—10-3 Indicate errors in use of terminal punctuation 10-4—10-7 Indicate errors in use of the comma 10-8—10-11 Indicate errors in use of the comma 10-12—10-15 Indicate errors in use of the comma 10-16 Indicate errors in use of the comma 10-17 Indicate errors in use of the comma 10-18 Indicate errors in use of the comma 10-19 Indicate errors in use of the comma 10-20 Indicate errors in use of the comma 10-21 Indicate errors in use of the comma 10-22 Indicate errors in use of the comma 10-23 Spelling Applications	P-1—P-4 Indicate errors in terminal punctuation, comma usage, and spelling Job 1 Proofread a business letter Job 2 Proofread printed copy against a rough draft Job 3 Proofread copy Job 4 Proofread an e-mail message Computerized Proofreading, Job 5 Proofread a memo *Computerized Proofreading, Job 6 Proofread advertising copy

*Optional template CD activities appear in the Instructor's Manual beginning on page 29.

Introduction

Chapter	Checkpoints	Applications
11. Punctuation Errors, Part 2	11-1—11-4 Indicate errors in use of the comma and semicolon 11-5 —11-9 Indicate errors in use of the comma, semicolon, and colon 11-10 —11-16 Indicate errors in use of the apostrophe 11-17—11-22 Indicate errors in use of quotation marks, the underscore, and italics 11-23—11-28 Indicate errors in use of the dash 11-29—11-34 Indicate errors in use of parentheses and brackets 11-35 Spelling Applications	P-1—P-4 Indicate errors in punctuation and spelling Job 1 Proofread an advertisement Job 2 Proofread a calendar of events Job 3 Proofread a letter Computerized Proofreading, Job 4 Proofread and revise a travel article *Computerized Proofreading, Job 5 Proofread a press release
12. Capitalization Errors	12-1, 12-2 Indicate capitalization errors 12-3, 12-4 Indicate capitalization errors 12-5—12-7 Indicate capitalization errors 12-8 Indicate capitalization errors 12-9, 12-10 Indicate capitalization errors 12-11 Indicate capitalization errors 12-12, 12-13 Indicate capitalization errors 12-14, 12-15 Indicate capitalization errors 12-16—12-18 Indicate capitalization errors 12-19 Spelling Applications	P-1—P-3 Indicate errors in capitalization P-4 Internet activity Job 1 Proofread an e-mail message Job 2 Proofread a bulletin board notice Job 3 Proofread a letter Job 4 Proofread a class schedule Computerized Proofreading, Job 5 Proofread a course announcement *Computerized Proofreading, Job 6 Proofread a memorandum
13. Editing for Content	13-1 Indicate incorrect facts 13-2 Indicate inconsistencies 13-3 Indicate missing information 13-4 Spelling Applications	P-1—P-3 Indicate errors in content and spelling Job 1 Proofread an invoice Job 2 Proofread a letter Job 3 Proofread an expense report Computerized Proofreading, Job 4 Edit a report *Computerized Proofreading, Job 5 Proofread a business letter
14. Editing for Conciseness	14-1 Indicate use of clichés and imprecise words 14-2, 14-3 Indicate use of obsolete terms 14-4 Change passive to active voice 14-5 Spelling Applications	P-1—P-4 Indicate errors in use of clichés, obsolete expressions, redundancies, passive voice, and spelling Job 1 Proofread a form letter Job 2 Proofread a memo Job 3 Proofread an e-mail message Computerized Proofreading, Job 4 Prepare a letter *Computerized Proofreading, Job 5 Proofread a business letter
15. Editing for Clarity	15-1, 15-2 Proofread for misplaced and dangling modifiers 15-3, 15-4 Proofread for nonparallel structures 15-5 Substitute simple words for more difficult words 15-6 Substitute strong verbs for weak verbs 15-7 Spelling Applications	P-1—P-3 Indicate errors in parallelism, misplaced and dangling modifiers, and complex words Job 1 Proofread a memo Job 2 Proofread two invoices Job 3 Proofread and edit a letter Computerized Proofreading, Job 4 Proofread and edit a letter *Computerized Proofreading, Job 5 Proofread a memo

*Optional template CD activities appear in the Instructor's Manual beginning on page 29.

GENERAL TEACHING SUGGESTIONS

Although instruction takes place in a variety of learning environments and no simple teaching recipe exists, these teaching tips have proven effective in educational research on classroom practice. You may select those ideas that are most appropriate for your students and for their instructional settings.

Tips for Student Success

Design your learning activities to recognize and respect the variation in student talents. Most students can be above average in some or all aspects of the course if their learning styles and strengths are identified and developed. Make students aware that people learn in different ways but that all have talents. Help students to respect one another's differences. Building student self-confidence promotes student success.

Teaching strategies and activities for each chapter should address different learning styles. When providing feedback to students, encourage them by noting items that are particularly good as well as areas needing improvement. Focus on major strengths and areas for improvement rather than calling attention to every error. Look for and build on each student's strengths.

Variety is the "spice of life" and the key to a successful class. By implementing the suggestions in this section, you will add spice to your class:

- Vary your instructional pattern. Use lecture and discussion. Use PowerPoint, the chalkboard, the overhead projector, and the opaque projector. If equipment is available, create messages using image display equipment.

- Encourage students to purchase and use a reference manual. (Using a reference manual is emphasized throughout the text.)

- Share with the class printed text you have found that contains errors, and encourage students to bring in printed text they have found containing errors.

- Invite former students to speak to the class about the types of messages they prepare in their jobs. Ask them to discuss the amount of time they spend proofreading and editing and the level of importance these skills command in their jobs.

- For some projects, allow students to collaborate. Have them work in groups of two or three to encourage careful proofreading.

- Have students use both spell check and grammar check features of word processing software.

- Use your creativity, talent, and experience to create proofreading and editing situations to supplement those in the text.

Introduction

Student Learning Styles

Some students are visual learners. These students need to see the information in books, on paper, on the chalkboard, on transparencies, or through other visual media. They may have difficulty with oral instructions; therefore, you should write directions as well as verbalize them. You may also ask the students to write the directions as you give them. Visual learners study best by taking and reviewing notes or marking important text sections for review. They make lists to remember items; a visual cue helps them remember a concept. Bulletin boards and posters, worksheets, reading activities, cartoons, illustrations, and demonstrations assist learning. Calling attention to the side margin notes in each chapter of the text will benefit the visual learner.

Listening is the best channel for the auditory learner. Class discussions, teacher lectures, guest speakers, oral questioning, mnemonic devices, peer tutoring, and oral presentation of directions and important concepts are beneficial teaching strategies. Allowing students to work together to read assignments to each other or breaking into small discussion groups helps the auditory learner. Have some assignments that groups of students can complete as a team.

Learning by doing is effective with most students; however, it is even more important for the kinesthetic or psychomotor learner. Teaching strategies designed for the kinesthetic learner include demonstrations intermixed with students performing the same process step by step, field trips relevant to the learning content, opportunities to move around in the classroom to work with other students or to work at the board, hands-on experiences with equipment such as a microcomputer, concrete examples of how content applies in daily life, and role playing or simulations.

Cooperative Learning

Used in addition to independent work activities, cooperative learning activities for specific projects or for small group discussions promote collaborative effort and teamwork. These skills are valuable in the workforce. Some students learn better by working with others; other students retain information better when working alone. Although the tasks of proofreading and editing are, for the most part, performed individually, as a learning experience, both group and individual activities have their place as teaching strategies. These elements promote effective group activities:

1. Group structure generally includes a mix of ability levels, and role assignments are made for specific responsibilities such as leader, recorder, and group facilitator.

2. Specify desired behavior to the groups; for example, encourage everyone to participate; listen carefully to what others are saying; check to see that all group members understand items discussed and can support the answers developed by the group; criticize ideas, not people; and use each person's name when addressing one another.

Use of Examples and Nonexamples

Student understanding of concepts and principles can be developed through examples and illustrations—not only of what *is* but also of what *is not*. For example, when teaching that correct sentence construction requires parallel wording for similar ideas, an example would be a sentence with correct parallelism; a sentence that is incorrect in terms of parallelism is a nonexample.

Student Evaluation

A helpful technique for improving proofreading and editing skill is to arrange some time for students to work in pairs to read each other's work and to look for errors that have been missed in the proofreading process. Providing a fully proofed and edited copy for students to use as a key gives a different angle to the proofreading process.

Assignment and course grading procedures should, of course, be based on the preferences of the individual instructor. Regardless of the grading scheme you choose, inform students of how they will be evaluated BEFORE they complete their first assignment.

Using a percentage system allows you to assign points that can be translated into a letter grade. If you wish to try a point system, consider the following:

- 100% for documents that contain no undetected errors

- 85% for documents that contain one or two undetected errors

- 80% for documents that contain three undetected errors

- 75% for documents that contain four undetected errors

- 70% for documents that contain five undetected errors

- no points for documents that contain more than five undetected errors

For COURSE GRADES, use your school's standards or the following percentages of total possible points OR highest points earned:

A	92%	B+	88%	C+	78%	D+	68%
A−	90%	B	82%	C	72%	D	62%
		B−	80%	C−	70%	D−	60%

Using a 2-6-2 grouping within each set gives recognition to the + and − portions of the grade ranges.

Introduction

CHAPTER 1: Proofreading for Quality Control

CLASSROOM STRATEGIES AND LEARNING ACTIVITIES

Chapter 1 defines proofreading and editing and gives techniques for developing these skills.

What Are Proofreading and Editing?

Help students understand the distinction between these two processes.

Importance of Proofreading and Editing

Motivate students to develop the habit of proofreading and to learn the processes of proofreading and editing by discussing business situations where students' written work will be read and their communication skills judged by others.

Proofreading Techniques

- Teach the three-step process of proofreading. It will be emphasized throughout the text.

- Discuss source documents. Ask students how they can find their own source documents when none are provided. Provide examples of source documents—company documents, letterheads, business cards, brochures, web sites, and phone books and other directories.

- Discuss team proofreading, especially pointing out situations where the method would be applicable. You could provide a legal description from a real estate document to demonstrate this method.

COMPUTERIZED PROOFREADING ACTIVITIES

Chapter 1 contains no computerized proofreading activities. These activities begin in Chapter 2.

LEARNING OBJECTIVES

- Define proofreading and editing.
- Explain the importance of proofreading.
- Explain the various methods of proofreading.

CHAPTER 2: Keyboarding Errors

TRANSPARENCY MASTERS

Transparency Masters 2-1 and 2-2 should be used to show proofreading symbols.

Transparency Master 2-3 may be used before the lecture or as a summary to cover the key points in Chapter 2.

CLASSROOM STRATEGIES AND LEARNING ACTIVITIES

In Chapter 2 students learn how to use proofreading symbols to show errors on a hard copy. For some students, this may be a new "language" they have never seen before. Introduce each mark by identifying it and demonstrating how to write it.

Keyboarding Errors of Omissions, Additions, and Misstrokes

- Introduce the insert symbol by name: caret. You might ask students to look up the word *caret* in the dictionary. Demonstrate how the caret is drawn beneath and between characters and words where an insertion of a character or word is needed and that the insertion is written above the existing text.

- Explain how the pound sign is often used in proofreading to indicate space.

- Introduce the close-up symbol, and explain that it is used only to close up spaces within a word and between words to bring the two words together. It is not used to delete extra spaces between words.

- Introduce the combined use of the delete symbol and the close-up symbol. This symbol is used when a deletion is made within a word and the word needs to remain solid. Compare that to when a space is needed after a deletion, such as deleting a hyphen in *word-processing* (to make *word processing*) or deleting the *d* in *linedup* (to create *line up*).

- Instruct students to use the proofreading symbol for changing a char-acter instead of the delete proofreading symbol to indicate changes in

The Basics of Proofreading: A Programmed Approach Instructor's Manual

characters. The delete proofreading symbol takes up too much room above the text to insert the new character(s) or text.

Keyboarding Errors in Figures, Enumerations, and Dates

- Bring hard cover stock (perhaps cut in half or in quarters) to class. Illustrate how a card like this can be used effectively to read down and across text and numerical lists. Discuss the differences in proofreading text and numerical data.

- Checkpoint 2-5 is the first project using a source document. Review what a source document is, and ask students for examples.

Transposition Errors

Emphasize that proofreaders often use the transposition proofreading symbol for words and phrases in addition to characters and numbers. Encourage students to write this symbol carefully, making sure they have transposed the correct characters or words.

Rough Draft Applications

Introduce the proofreading symbols for move copy, let it stand (or stet), and change copy. Explain that the symbol for move copy can be drawn around small pieces of text (such as words) and large pieces of text (such as sentences or paragraphs). For discussion, ask students why the symbol for let it stand is important. Prompt them to discuss how a proofreader might delete or strike through a piece of text and then have a change of mind.

Spelling Applications

Emphasize to students the importance of learning how to spell the list of spelling words. Discuss the capabilities and limitations of the spell check function in word processing programs. Emphasize that regardless of the availability of a spell check function, a student must be able to produce business documents that are free of spelling errors. Remind students to look for these words in their chapter proofreading exercises.

COMPUTERIZED PROOFREADING ACTIVITIES

Job 4 is a page from an employee manual that includes a table with dollar amounts. Job 5 is a page from a financial brochure. In addition to the edits written on the handout, this job also contains unmarked errors for students to find.

See page 31 in this Instructor's Manual for the handout that accompanies Chapter 2 Computerized Proofreading Application, Job 5, which appears on the template CD-ROM. The solution for this application appears on page 47 of this Instructor's Manual.

CHAPTER 3: Abbreviation Errors

TRANSPARENCY MASTERS

Transparency Master 3-1 should be used to illustrate proofreading symbols. No symbols are provided. You can show students the correct symbol for each meaning by writing the symbol in the left column. Then you can apply the symbol to correct each sentence in the right column.

Transparency Masters 3-2 and 3-3 may be used during the lecture to explain and demonstrate abbreviation concepts and proofreading symbols.

Transparency Master 3-4 may be used before the lecture or as a summary to cover the key points in Chapter 3.

CLASSROOM STRATEGIES AND LEARNING ACTIVITIES

Chapter 3 presents abbreviations, initialisms, and acronyms. Many abbreviation rules are presented but only three proofreading symbols. These three symbols will correct most abbreviation errors.

Abbreviation Errors

- Illustrate the three proofreading symbols presented. Explain that a circle surrounds the period so that it can be easily seen on the page. Discuss the importance of the proofreading symbol for closing up space and what might be interpreted if this symbol were omitted.

- Carefully teach the use of personal names and titles since they are common in all business communications.

- Ask students to demonstrate how to write with personal names the professional designations or academic degrees they will encounter in their career fields. For example, students entering the legal profession need to know the meanings of and how to write the titles *ALS* (Accredited Legal Secretary), *Certified PLS* (Certified Professional Legal Secretary), and *Esq.* (Esquire, a term attorneys use to address each other). This research could be conducted as a team project with groups of students who plan to enter the same career fields.

- Discuss the difference between formal text, such as correspondence and reports, and informal text, such as e-mail messages. Checkpoints 3-6—3-8 contain the words *facsimile* and *electronic mail* that should, in this situation, be abbreviated *fax* and *e-mail*.

- Introduce the use of the Internet as a research tool for proofreaders. Have students find sites that describe agency and government names by searching for the acronyms or the names.

- To teach correct addressing, explain the difference between addresses in text, inside addresses on correspondence, and addresses on envelopes. For information on addressing envelopes, you can obtain printed materials from the U.S. Postal Service for distribution in class or refer students to the USPS web site at http://usps.com/.

- Challenge students to expand the list of shortened word forms listed in 3-7 so they will recognize that these word forms are not abbreviations. This exercise could be done in teams.

Spelling Applications

Ten spelling words are presented. Remind students to look for these words in their chapter proofreading exercises.

COMPUTERIZED PROOFREADING ACTIVITIES

Job 4 is an interoffice memorandum. Students should check the hand-written notes against the information contained in the memo. Job 5 is an e-mail message. It contains errors not marked for the students to find.

See page 32 in this Instructor's Manual for the handout that accompanies Chapter 3 Computerized Proofreading Application, Job 5, which appears on the template CD-ROM. The solution for this application appears on page 47 of this Instructor's Manual.

CHAPTER 4: Word Division Errors

TRANSPARENCY MASTERS

Transparency Masters 4-1 and 4-2 may be used as an exercise to review the word division rules. After presenting each rule, you might ask students to indicate where to divide the words listed.

Transparency Master 4-3 may be used before the lecture or as a summary to cover the key points in Chapter 4.

CLASSROOM STRATEGIES AND LEARNING ACTIVITIES

Chapter 4 presents guidelines for correct word division and instruction for when not to divide words. The chapter presents a new proofreading symbol for inserting a hyphen and shows how to correct an improper word division. In addition, a forward slash symbol (/) is used in this chapter to illustrate where a word division would occur in the following circumstances: (1) words that contain internal hyphens, such as hyphenated compound words; (2) word groups that do not contain hyphens, such as dates; and (3) URLs, e-mail addresses, and extremely long numbers that do not contain hyphens. In these instances word division may occur but a hyphen should not be inserted.

Correct Word Division

- Discuss the differences among soft, regular, and hard hyphens. Point out the marginal note on page 37 that explains how to create these hyphens using Word and WordPerfect. Also, discuss the hard space; review the marginal note on page 38. Ask students with other software to find out how to insert hard hyphens and hard spaces using their programs.

- Bring word division books and/or dictionaries to class to illustrate syllabication and application of word division rules.

- Assign teams to search various types of documents for word division. Have students note the differences in newspaper articles, magazine articles, business letters, legal documents, and advertisements (including classified ads). Questions for discussion might include whether correct word division rules were followed and if not, why not.

When to Avoid Word Division

Encourage students to develop the habit of always keying a hard space where needed (refer to 4-12 and 4-13), not just when the words are being keyed at the end of a line. Discuss how revisions to text change line endings and what those changes might mean to word groups that should not be divided.

Spelling Applications

Ten spelling words are presented. Remind students to look for these words in their chapter proofreading exercises.

COMPUTERIZED PROOFREADING ACTIVITIES

Job 5 is a business letter to a supporter of the nonprofit organization used in the chapter. Students are asked to proofread the letter and compare it to form paragraphs. In Job 6 students must proofread a handwritten list of donated auction items against a keyed copy.

See page 33 in this Instructor's Manual for the handout that accompanies Chapter 4 Computerized Proofreading Application, Job 6, which appears on the template CD-ROM. The solution for this application appears on page 48 of this Instructor's Manual.

CHAPTER 5: Number Expression Errors

TRANSPARENCY MASTERS

Transparency Masters 5-1 through 5-4 are exercises to develop skill in proofreading for correct numerical expression. You can use the transparency masters in different ways. After reviewing each rule, you might demonstrate the proofreading symbol that corrects the error in the text. Or after reviewing each rule, you might ask students to make the necessary correction(s) to the text.

CLASSROOM STRATEGIES AND LEARNING ACTIVITIES

Chapter 5 presents guidelines for correct expression of numbers and provides instruction for proofreading text that contains numerical data. Be sure to explain the two styles of numerical expression: figure style and word style. This chapter includes applications that can be solved using either words or figures. Discuss these situations in class so students can develop skill in determining which style to use in different circumstances.

Basic Rules

- Understand the difference between numbers that are emphasized within text and those that are not. The emphasis placed on a number often determines whether figure style or word style is used.

LEARNING OBJECTIVES

- Identify errors in the expression of numbers.
- Identify keyboarding errors in numerical calculations.
- Use appropriate proofreading symbols to indicate changes in text.
- Spell correctly a list of commonly misspelled words.

- Bring in samples of correspondence and other types of business documents for a class project that can be done in teams. Have students review the documents and highlight every use of a number, whether figure style or word style, and check the number style for correct expression. Are the expressions of numbers correct? Are they consistent within the document? Are they consistent among documents?

Specific Rules

- Remind students that most pieces of correspondence contain an inside address and that most addresses have numbers as part of the street name. Therefore, students must be able to apply number rules to addresses.

- Encourage students to develop the habit of always keying a hard space where needed between nouns and numbers (refer to 5-10).

- Because consistency is often stressed, students may include (1) a colon and two zeros after an on-the-hour time (5:00) if another colon is used in the same sentence or (2) a decimal and two zeros after an even dollar amount ($10.00) if another dollar amount using a decimal is included in the same sentence. Discuss the proper numerical expression of times and dollar amounts, and emphasize that colons or decimals followed by two zeros are not necessary.

- Remind students that just as using correct expressions for numbers is important, proofreading for correct numbers is critical. Discuss identifying and using source documents to check numbers.

Special Rules

- Discuss consistency of number style within a document. For instance, a writer may or may not use a comma with a four-digit number. Whatever style the writer chooses, though, he or she should be consistent.

- Stress the importance of making the meaning of numbers clear and of verifying numbers and any calculations in a document.

Spelling Applications

Ten spelling words are presented. Remind students to look for these words in their chapter proofreading exercises.

COMPUTERIZED PROOFREADING ACTIVITIES

Job 5 is a journal article that students must proofread and format. In Job 6 students proofread an on-screen e-mail message against an information sheet.

See page 34 in this Instructor's Manual for the handout that accompanies Chapter 5 Computerized Proofreading Application, Job 6, which appears on the template CD-ROM. The solution for this application appears on page 48 of this Instructor's Manual.

CHAPTER 6: Format Errors

TRANSPARENCY MASTERS

Use Transparency Masters 6-1 and 6-2 to demonstrate the use of the many proofreading symbols introduced in this chapter. Symbols are provided in the left column.

Use Transparency Masters 6-3, 6-4, and 6-5 to display letter formats. Use Transparency Master 6-6 to display memo format. Use Transparency Master 6-7 to display report format.

CLASSROOM STRATEGIES AND LEARNING ACTIVITIES

Chapter 6 presents the standard formats for business letters, memos, e-mail messages, and reports. Proofing for format errors includes checking vertical spacing, horizontal spacing, and alignment as well as checking for missing document components, such as an enclosure notation. Students learn 12 new proofreading symbols to use in correcting format errors.

Importance of Format

Illustrate the 12 proofreading symbols presented. Point out the directions for SS, DS, TS, and QS explained in the marginal note on page 72.

Letter Format

- Share with students examples of business letters, or ask students to bring samples to class. Discuss the styles used in these examples.
- Remind students that they can and should develop a personal letterhead for their own business correspondence. The letterhead should include a complete return address, a personal title and name, and a professional title, if appropriate.

Business Letter Styles

- Discuss the letter styles presented in the chapter to ensure that students understand the differences. Stress the importance of not mixing and matching styles, but being consistent within a prescribed style.

- Highlight the differences between block style and modified block style, and emphasize that paragraphs are indented only in a modified block style letter.

- Ask volunteers to identify each part of a letter, describing the spacing requirements.

Letter Placement

- Refer to the sample letters you or the students provided, discussing placement of the text on the paper. A "bad example" would offer a good opportunity to discuss with students how to improve letter placement.

- No proofreading symbol is given for moving text up or down on the page; discuss how this change might be indicated on a letter.

Memorandum Format

Point out to students that most word processing programs include memo templates. Have students explore their own software programs to see what memo forms are available.

E-mail Format

Most students are familiar with e-mail software and formats from their personal use. Discuss how business messages differ from personal messages and why a greater degree of formality is required for both internal and external business e-mail messages. Also, discuss the confidentiality issues that e-mail messages present.

Report Format

- Emphasize that report formats vary widely. The formats presented in this chapter cover the fundamental issues of margins, title page, headings, and text organization. With these basics any editor or proofreader should be able to identify errors or inconsistencies in a report.

- Discuss when a report may include the optional elements presented in the chapter and why these elements would be helpful to a reader.

- Tell students that a writer has the responsibility of citing his or her sources, whether those sources are print, multimedia, personal interview or research, or online. Information on the Internet is usually copyrighted and, therefore, must be cited. Even if the contents of a web site do not appear to be copyrighted, writers are still responsible for crediting the information used. Citing web sites can be complicated, but the general rule is to provide enough information so that readers can gain access to the site if they so desire. Documentation style guides are available that cover citation format for all types of web sites.

- If available, bring in copies of an ALA, APA, or MLA manual to show students the complexity and detail of citation formats.

- Have students search the Internet for university writing labs that discuss report writing and citation styles. Refer students to Purdue University's Online Writing Lab (OWL) at http://owl.english.purdue.edu/ to begin their search.

Spelling Applications

Ten frequently misspelled words are presented. Remind students to look for these words in the chapter proofreading exercises.

COMPUTERIZED PROOFREADING ACTIVITIES

Job 5 is an interoffice memorandum. Students should check the memo on the template CD-ROM against the handwritten version. The handwritten version contains errors; the keyed version replicates some of those errors and introduces new ones. Job 6 is a long business letter. Students are provided a source document, which consists of notes taken by the letter writer prior to her keying the letter. The notes contain some abbreviations but are otherwise correct.

See page 35 in this Instructor's Manual for the handout that accompanies Chapter 6 Computerized Proofreading Application, Job 6, which appears on the template CD-ROM. The solution for this application appears on page 49 of this Instructor's Manual.

CHAPTER 7: Grammar Errors: Sentence Structure

TRANSPARENCY MASTERS

Use Transparency Master 7-1 to summarize the parts of a sentence. Students must know sentence parts to create grammatically correct sentences.

Use Transparency Masters 7-2 through 7-5 to illustrate subject-verb agreement. The answers to the sample sentences are given at the bottom of each master. Demonstrate proofreading symbols to make corrections to the sentences.

Use Transparency Master 7-6 to discuss the three types of sentence faults discussed in Chapter 7. The sample sentences may be corrected several ways, but only one suggested answer is given.

CLASSROOM STRATEGIES AND LEARNING ACTIVITIES

Chapter 7 discusses grammatically correct sentences by first explaining parts of a sentence, then covering subject-verb agreement, and finally illustrating three types of sentence faults. No new proofreading symbols are introduced in this chapter.

Parts of a Sentence

Be sure students understand subjects and predicates and other parts of a sentence before presenting the remainder of the chapter. These concepts relate to the rest of Chapter 7 and also to Chapter 8.

Subject–Verb Agreement

- Most of the sample sentences in Chapter 7 sound incorrect when the subject and verb do not agree. However, the more complex the sentence, the more difficult subject-verb agreement may be. The key is to locate true subjects and verbs and not to rely on what sounds correct.

- Checkpoint 7-1, 7-2 asks students to label nouns, pronouns, verbs, and linking verbs. The remaining Checkpoint exercises do not ask students to label sentence parts. However, you could take the exercises a step further and ask students to identify true subjects and verbs by labeling the sentence parts in addition to correcting the sentences.

- Have students write sample sentences or a simple document (such as a memo), creating subject-verb errors within the sentences. Have each student exchange the document with another student, asking him or her to use proofreading symbols to correct the errors.

- Students often have trouble with collective nouns. A project that works for large and small groups is to have students brainstorm to create lists of collective nouns. You could expand the project by having the group(s) write sentences in both singular and plural form using their list of collective nouns.

Sentence Faults

Discuss each of the three sentence faults presented, explaining how to identify and correct each fault. You can discuss various ways to correct

LEARNING OBJECTIVES

- Describe the parts of a complete sentence.
- Create subject and verb agreement.
- Identify and correct sentence structure faults.
- Use appropriate proofreading symbols to indicate changes in text.
- Spell correctly a list of commonly misspelled words.

The Basics of Proofreading: A Programmed Approach Instructor's Manual

sentence faults, including using punctuation that has not yet been presented in this text. However, each sentence fault can be corrected using principles covered in Chapter 7.

Spelling Applications

Ten frequently misspelled words are presented. Remind students to look for these words in the chapter proofreading exercises.

COMPUTERIZED PROOFREADING ACTIVITIES

Job 4 is a business letter prepared from a handwritten note. The handwritten note is the source document, and the document on the template CD-ROM contains errors. Formatting instructions are given to the students. Job 5 is a memo. A handwritten note is provided as a source document for some of the information in the memo.

See page 36 in this Instructor's Manual for the handout that accompanies Chapter 7 Computerized Proofreading Application, Job 5, which appears on the template CD-ROM. The solution for this application appears on page 49 of this Instructor's Manual.

CHAPTER 8: Grammar Errors: Pronoun Agreement and Selection

TRANSPARENCY MASTERS

Use Transparency Master 8-1 to begin a discussion of pronouns. You could photocopy this master and distribute it to students as a handout for their reference and study.

Use Transparency Masters 8-2, 8-3, and 8-4 to illustrate pronoun choice. Demonstrate proofreading symbols to correct pronouns in sentences.

Use Transparency Master 8-5 to illustrate gender-neutral language. Demonstrate ways to improve pronoun selection in sentences.

CLASSROOM STRATEGIES AND LEARNING ACTIVITIES

Chapter 8 discusses pronouns and how the choice of pronouns affects grammar. One new proofreading symbol is introduced in this chapter. The query author proofreading symbol obviously can be used for any type of query, but it is presented in this chapter so it can be used if a pronoun reference is unclear.

LEARNING OBJECTIVES

- Identify and correct errors in pronoun-antecedent agreement.
- Identify and correct errors in pronoun case.
- Write sentences with gender-neutral language.
- Use appropriate proofreading symbols to indicate changes in text.
- Spell correctly a list of commonly misspelled words.

Pronoun–Antecedent Agreement

- Many terms are defined in Chapter 8, such as *antecedent* in this section. Be sure students understand antecedents so that they can make pronouns agree with antecedents.

- Give special emphasis to collective nouns and indefinite pronouns as antecedents. Refer students to the lists of indefinite pronouns in Chapter 7.

- Checkpoint 8-1 requires students to label antecedents prior to making pronouns agree with their antecedents. You could use this same labeling idea throughout the remaining Checkpoint exercises to reinforce sentence parts and to help students develop skill in identifying pronoun errors.

Pronoun Cases

- Discuss each of the three pronoun cases. Remind students to apply their knowledge of sentence parts when choosing the correct pronoun case.

- Encourage students to memorize the nominative, objective, and possessive case pronouns.

- As a class or group project, assign students to create lists of prepositions. Students who can recognize prepositions easily will be able to recognize objects of prepositions and thus correctly choose objective case pronouns as objects.

- Another term defined in Chapter 8 is *infinitive*. Once students see that an infinitive is simply a verb form, they can apply the proper pronoun case.

- Possessive pronouns are seldom troublesome—except for those students who want to insert apostrophes and for those who fail to recognize gerunds. An illustrative way to teach gerunds is to have students write sentences with action verbs. Then have students write (or exchange papers with another student to write) new sentences using the same action verbs as gerunds. As a further step, have students place possessive pronouns immediately before the gerunds. You can begin this exercise with the following example:

    I was *singing* in the shower this morning. (as an action verb)

    Singing is what I love to do. (as a gerund)

    My *singing* has brought me neither fame nor fortune.

    (as a gerund modified by a possessive pronoun)

- If students struggle with *who* and *whom*, create or have students create clauses that include *who/whom* choices. Have them identify the sentence parts. Once they see the subject-verb-object order, they will be able to choose the correct pronoun case.

Gender–Neutral Language

Find or have students find newspaper or magazine articles that include examples of pronoun use when a person's gender is unknown. These types of examples can be easily found in advice columns or articles written about child care. If time permits, you can make these articles a part of the discussion or you can have students write a short analysis of whether the article was well written or poorly written with regard to pronoun use.

Spelling Applications

Ten frequently misspelled words are presented. Remind students to look for these words in the chapter proofreading exercises.

COMPUTERIZED PROOFREADING ACTIVITIES

Job 4 is an e-mail message. The handwritten note is the source document, and the document on the template CD-ROM still contains errors. Give students instructions for how this document should look in final form. A memo heading such as TO, FROM, DATE, and SUBJECT is sufficient since students fill in these fields when using e-mail software.

Job 5 is a personal business letter written in response to the letter in Job 1. See page 37 in this Instructor's Manual for the handout that accompanies Chapter 8 Computerized Proofreading Application, Job 5, which appears on the template CD-ROM. The solution for this application appears on page 50 of this Instructor's Manual.

CHAPTER 9: Errors in Words Often Confused

TRANSPARENCY MASTERS

Use Transparency Masters 9-1 through 9-5 to have students work through the choices of words often confused. You also could duplicate the transparency masters and have students use them as worksheet activities. The answers to the sample sentences are given at the bottom of each master.

CLASSROOM STRATEGIES AND LEARNING ACTIVITIES

Chapter 9 presents words that cause difficulty for many business communicators. Proofreaders should be aware of these difficult words so they can watch for them while proofreading for context. No new proofreading symbols are introduced in this chapter.

Importance of Distinguishing Between Similar Words

- Encourage students to use a current dictionary to look up words they are not familiar with while working on this chapter.

- Have students write correct sentences using the words presented. You could instruct them to write sentences in the order in which the words are presented in the chapter. You also could ask students to write a memo or letter on a certain topic, instructing the students to insert words from the chapter into their memos or letters.

- For an assignment that can be done in teams, have students create additional exercises similar to the Checkpoint exercises in the chapter using word groups not already covered. Then have the teams exchange exercises and work on these additional word groups.

Words Deserving Special Consideration

- No Checkpoint exercise is provided for this section. You could have students create their own Checkpoint exercises. Students could incorporate the words presented in this section into their memos or letters (described above), or they could write sentences or paragraphs using this group of special words.

- Discuss other words that cannot logically be compared, such as the word *unique* presented in the chapter. Begin your discussion with the words *round, square, straight, dead, never,* and *perfect;* ask students if they can add to this list. Then present the special adverbs *more nearly, hardly, almost,* and *virtually* that should be used in combination with words such as *unique* when these words are being used in comparisons.

Spelling Applications

Ten frequently misspelled words are presented. Remind students to look for these words in the chapter proofreading exercises.

COMPUTERIZED PROOFREADING ACTIVITIES

Job 4 is a memo that includes a table of statistical information. The table of statistical information is provided as a source document to proofread against. Job 5 is advertising copy related to real estate. Another document containing accurate information is provided as a source document.

See page 38 in this Instructor's Manual for the handout that accompanies Chapter 9 Computerized Proofreading Applications, Job 5, which appears on the template CD-ROM. The solution for this application appears on page 50 of this Instructor's Manual.

CHAPTER 10: Punctuation Errors, Part 1

TRANSPARENCY MASTERS

Use Transparency Masters 10-1 through 10-6 to discuss and illustrate terminal punctuation and the comma. Involve students in completing the exercises. The answers to the sample sentences are given at the bottom of each master.

CLASSROOM STRATEGIES AND LEARNING ACTIVITIES

Chapter 10 presents punctuation that is used in every sentence—terminal punctuation. The chapter also presents the most common punctuation mark, the comma. While this text is not all-inclusive in its coverage of commas, the main issues that trouble students and writers are presented here. New proofreading symbols are introduced for inserting and deleting the period, the question mark, the exclamation point, and the comma.

Importance of Correct Punctuation

While other punctuation marks are mentioned in Chapter 10, only terminal punctuation marks and the comma are discussed. Remind students that other marks of punctuation will be discussed in Chapter 11.

LEARNING OBJECTIVES

- Identify errors in terminal punctuation.
- Identify errors in using commas to separate words.
- Identify errors in using commas to separate sentence parts.
- Identify errors in using commas with essential and nonessential sentence elements.
- Use appropriate proofreading symbols to indicate changes in text.
- Spell correctly a list of commonly misspelled words.

Terminal Punctuation

The three punctuation marks used in standard English are presented. Explain the use of the period for indirect questions and polite requests and the use of the question mark for statements phrased as questions, as these applications present the most problems for students.

Internal Punctuation—The Comma

Explain the severity of the break that commas give. Commas are internal punctuation; therefore, their break is not as strong as terminal punctuation. Although examples are given in Chapter 10 using commas, parentheses or dashes could also be used. Help students understand that writers must choose how strong a break they want to achieve. While dashes emphasize text and parentheses de-emphasize text, commas give neutral emphasis to text.

Using the Comma to Separate Words

Chapter 10 points out that commas should be used to provide clarity to writing; however, emphasize that commas should be used to provide clarity within the confines of accepted comma rules. Students should be able to cite a rule for each comma they insert.

Using the Comma to Separate Sentence Parts

- The different sentence structures are presented so students can identify them in order to punctuate them correctly.

- Be sure students understand the difference between a compound sentence and a simple sentence with compound verbs. Provide examples and work through them with students.

- Introductory text is sometimes troublesome for students. To demonstrate how to use commas with introductory text, create a simple sentence. Then have students write a short introductory prepositional phrase, an introductory verbal phrase, and an introductory dependent clause for the sentence. You can begin this exercise with the following example:

  I plan to be an excellent proofreader.

  Before graduation I plan to be an excellent proofreader.

  Learning more each day, I plan to be an excellent proofreader.

  Because proofreading is an important skill, I plan to be an excellent proofreader.

- You can continue this exercise to emphasize terminal dependent clauses that may or may not be introduced by a comma. Use the same example sentence.

I plan to be an excellent proofreader *because proofreading is an important skill.*

I plan to be an excellent proofreader, *if you think it is an important skill.*

Essential and Nonessential Elements

Point out that even though a sentence may be grammatically correct without the essential element, it is not complete in a comprehensive sense. Students may not understand this difference.

Spelling Applications

Ten frequently misspelled words are presented. Remind students to look for these words in the chapter proofreading exercises.

COMPUTERIZED PROOFREADING ACTIVITIES

Job 5 is a memo to office employees and Job 6 is advertising copy. Handwritten notes are provided as source documents.

See page 39 in this Instructor's Manual for the handout that accompanies Chapter 10 Computerized Proofreading Application, Job 6, which appears on the template CD-ROM. The solution for this application appears on page 51 of this Instructor's Manual.

CHAPTER 11: Punctuation Errors, Part 2

TRANSPARENCY MASTERS

Use Transparency Masters 11-1 through 11-8 to illustrate the use of semicolons, colons, apostrophes, quotation marks, underscores, dashes, and parentheses. The answers to the sample sentences are given at the bottom of each master.

CLASSROOM STRATEGIES AND LEARNING ACTIVITIES

Chapter 11 concludes coverage of punctuation marks. Most of the punctuation problems students will encounter in business writing are covered in Chapters 10 and 11. New proofreading symbols are introduced for inserting semicolons, colons, apostrophes, quotation marks, underscores, dashes, parentheses, and brackets.

LEARNING OBJECTIVES

- Detect errors in the use of these punctuation marks: semicolons, colons, apostrophes, quotation marks, underscores, dashes, parentheses, and brackets.

- Use appropriate proofreading symbols to indicate changes in text.

- Spell correctly a list of commonly misspelled words.

Punctuation to Clarify

Proofreading symbols are not presented for deleting or changing punctuation marks. Instruct students to delete a punctuation mark by drawing the delete sign and to change a punctuation mark by deleting the incorrect symbol and inserting the correct symbol. Also, point out to students that parentheses and brackets are not inserted using carets.

Semicolon

- Explain the difference between the coordinating conjunctions (*and, but, or,* and *nor*) and the adverbial conjunctions (*therefore, however, in the meantime,* and so on) so students can distinguish between the two and use the semicolon correctly.

- Have students gain practice at identifying the two kinds of conjunctions by writing compound sentences first using coordinating conjunctions and then changing the coordinating conjunctions to adverbial conjunctions. This exercise demonstrates that the sentence construction remains the same; only the punctuation changes.

Colon

- A common mistake students make using colons is to follow verbs and prepositions with colons. Discuss that even though verbs and prepositions may introduce lists, they should not be followed by colons unless the list is formatted vertically.

- A good exercise to demonstrate using a colon with lists—and not using a colon following verbs and prepositions—is to create a list; then introduce the list in a variety of ways. You can begin this exercise by creating a list of items students typically have in their backpacks. Ask students to write the list introduced by a verb, then a preposition, and then a colon.

    The items I have in my backpack *are* pens, computer disks, textbooks, and paper.

    My backpack is full *of* pens, computer disks, textbooks, and paper.

    The items I have in my backpack *are these* [or *are the following*]: pens, computer disks, textbooks, and paper.

Apostrophe

Possessives are briefly covered in Chapter 11 in the section on apostrophes. Refer students to a more in-depth coverage on possessives in an English textbook or a reference manual if this is a troublesome area for them.

Quotation Marks

- Be sure to point out placement of punctuation marks with quotation marks.

- Remind students not to confuse use of quotation marks for titles of articles or chapters with the underscore, which is used for titles of books or separately published works.

Underscore and Italics

Explain to students that underscores and italics mean the same thing and can be used interchangeably. However, students should be consistent with their use of underscores or italics within a document.

Dash

- Remind students that dashes are used to emphasize text.

- Continue with the exercise used in the discussion of colons by demonstrating the dash when a list comes before the introduction. Rewrite the sentence as follows:

  > Pens, computer disks, textbooks, and paper—these are the items I have in my backpack.

Parentheses

- Remind students that parentheses are used to de-emphasize text.

- Point out that even though a sentence may be grammatically correct without the nonessential element, it is not complete in a comprehensive sense. Students may not understand this difference.

Brackets

Carefully instruct students on the use of *sic*, as this is an editing symbol they may not have used or seen before.

Spelling Applications

Ten frequently misspelled words are presented. Remind students to look for these words in the chapter proofreading exercises.

COMPUTERIZED PROOFREADING ACTIVITIES

Job 4 is an article about travel in Georgia. Students can refer to Chapter 6 for reminders of how to set up an unbound report.

Job 5 is a press release. Handwritten notes are provided as a source document. See page 40 in this Instructor's Manual for the handout that accompanies Chapter 11 Computerized Proofreading Application, Job 5, which appears on the template CD-ROM. The solution for this application appears on pages 51 and 52 of this Instructor's Manual.

CHAPTER 12: Capitalization Errors

TRANSPARENCY MASTERS

Use Transparency Masters 12-1 through 12-6 to review the capitalization rules presented in this chapter. The transparency masters summarize the capitalization rules and provide example sentences with errors for students to correct.

CLASSROOM STRATEGIES AND LEARNING ACTIVITIES

Chapter 12 presents the main body of capitalization rules. As proofreaders and editors, students need to be familiar with capitalization rules. Emphasize to students that if they are unable to apply a rule to a capitalized word, then there is no need for capitalization. Students learn two basic proofreading symbols for correcting capitalization errors.

Functions of Capitalization

- Show students examples of direct marketing (i.e., junk mail) that use capitalization for emphasis. In some cases these documents are printed in all capital letters. Have students respond to the effect of these mailings, both in terms of visual impact and comprehension. As an extra activity after students have completed the chapter, have them proofread one of these documents and apply standard rules of capitalization.

- Have students experiment with their word processing programs to see if the spell check or grammar check programs detect errors in capitalization. Point out that the computer never replaces the knowledge and judgment of an accurate proofreader.

Sentences, Words, and Headings

- Discuss how using a dictionary and reference manual can aid a proofreader in making capitalization decisions. Discuss the differences between a dictionary and a reference manual and when one is a more appropriate resource than the other.

- Practice applying capitalization to names of articles and headings. Have students find the function on their word processors that changes the case of highlighted text to a title case. Most programs do not make distinctions among word types (verbs, prepositions, articles, and so on); therefore, all highlighted words are changed to title case. Bring students to the conclusion that they cannot rely on this software feature to provide error-free capitalization usage for names of articles and headings.

Names of Places and Things

Emphasize to students that most capitalization errors are made because a business communicator cannot distinguish between a general name and a specific name.

Additional Capitalization Rules

Remind students of the three-step process of proofreading and that they should proofread outlines and vertical lists as a separate step, checking capitalization in that separate step.

Spelling Applications

Ten frequently misspelled words are presented. Remind students to look for these words in the chapter proofreading exercises.

COMPUTERIZED PROOFREADING ACTIVITIES

Job 5 is an announcement. Students should check the memo on the template against the handwritten notes. The handwritten notes are accurate, but capitalization rules are not necessarily applied correctly. Other format errors also occur in the handwritten copy.

Job 6 is a memo. Students are provided a source document, which consists of a handwritten draft of the memo. The draft contains some errors. The document on the template CD-ROM replicates some of these errors, and other errors are introduced.

See page 41 in this Instructor's Manual for the handout that accompanies Chapter 12 Computerized Proofreading Application, Job 6, which appears on the template CD-ROM. The solution for this application appears on page 52 of this Instructor's Manual.

CHAPTER 13: Editing for Content

TRANSPARENCY MASTERS

Use Transparency Masters 13-1 and 13-2 to demonstrate the content issues presented in this chapter. You could show the transparencies and discuss the rules about which students raise questions, or you could distribute copies as handouts for students to work on individually or in groups.

CLASSROOM STRATEGIES AND LEARNING ACTIVITIES

Chapter 13 is the first of three chapters on editing. This chapter deals specifically with the content issues of incorrect facts, inconsistencies, and missing information. These errors raise questions for the author, or they raise questions for which the proofreader can find answers.

Editing for Content

Discuss the responsibilities of a proofreader, including when and how a proofreader should find answers to his or her own queries.

Incorrect Facts

- Discuss source documents and the extent to which a proofreader must rely on sources to obtain correct facts.

- Job 2 is a letter that includes a reference to this text. The letter contains an error when it states that Chapter 9 deals with formatting issues; the letter should reference Chapter 6. You could point out to the students that they possess the source document to check this fact, or you could let them figure it out on their own.

Inconsistencies

Discuss the three-step process of proofreading. In particular, discuss how proofreading names, numbers, and other special pieces of a document as a separate step would aid a proofreader in looking for inconsistencies within a document. For instance, the letter in Job 2 first states 93 percent, then 90 percent.

Missing Information

At times missing information will create a grammatically incorrect sentence, and a grammar check function may point this out to the proofreader. However, a grammatically incorrect sentence does not always result from missing information. The proofreader must read text carefully to make sure it makes sense.

The Basics of Proofreading: A Programmed Approach Instructor's Manual

Spelling Applications

Ten frequently misspelled words are presented. Remind students to look for these words in the chapter proofreading exercises.

COMPUTERIZED PROOFREADING ACTIVITIES

Job 4 is a report. Remind students to refer to Chapter 6 for format guidelines regarding reports.

Job 5 is a letter to a supplier. Students are provided a source document, which is a handwritten draft of the letter. The draft contains some errors. The document on the template CD-ROM replicates some of these errors, and some other errors are introduced.

See page 42 in this Instructor's Manual for the handout that accompanies Chapter 13 Computerized Proofreading Application, Job 5, which appears on the template CD-ROM. The solution for this application appears on page 53 of this Instructor's Manual.

CHAPTER 14: Editing for Conciseness

TRANSPARENCY MASTERS

Use Transparency Masters 14-1 and 14-2 to demonstrate how to edit for conciseness. You could show the transparencies to students and discuss options for editing, or you could distribute copies of the masters to students for extra practice either individually or in groups.

CLASSROOM STRATEGIES AND LEARNING ACTIVITIES

Like Chapter 13, Chapter 14 instructs students on how to edit text. Chapter 14 emphasizes the importance of conciseness with regard to business communications. The editing necessary to trim wordy and obsolete expressions is a step above simply proofreading for mechanical errors.

Clichés and Imprecise Words

Students can identify the clichés they have heard and may use. Often they think that because a cliché is understood, it is acceptable in business writing. Discuss how business writing is different from speaking or other forms of writing.

Obsolete and Redundant Expressions

Role-play situations where students are faced with preparing business documents for a supervisor or person of authority in an employment situation. If the originator uses obsolete expressions, should the student (employee) edit these? How should he or she handle the situation?

Passive Voice

- Discuss situations where passive voice is appropriate. Job 2 presents one such situation, where the office manager does not want to name the person who breeched confidentiality.

- Practice the example sentences and Checkpoint exercises, and create other sentences for students who need extra practice identifying passive voice. An effective exercise is to create sentences in active voice and then rewrite those sentences placing the subject after the verb or hiding the doer of the action. You can begin this exercise with the following examples:

Active	The instructor ordered lunch for all the students in the class.
Passive	Lunch was ordered by the instructor for all the students in the class.
	Lunch was ordered for all the students in the class.
Active	The students enjoyed the lunch.
Passive	The lunch was enjoyed by the students.
	The lunch was enjoyed.

Spelling Applications

Ten frequently misspelled words are presented. Remind students to look for these words in the chapter proofreading exercises.

COMPUTERIZED PROOFREADING ACTIVITIES

Job 4 is a letter enclosing a check. While concentrating on other proofreading and editing issues, students may forget to include an enclosure notation. Remind students to refer to the source document (handwritten note) from which the letter was prepared.

Job 5 is a letter to a person who has applied for a job at the firm. Students will use the corrected form letter from Job 1 for the reply and incorporate handwritten comments from a draft copy that appears in their text. Note that the handwritten comments include Ada Carlton's calculation that the applicant has seven years of office experience. This is a planted error; students should check the calculation as part of the proofreading process and find the error. Students will have to calculate the exact number of years using the dates on the résumé since this number obviously will change each year this text is used.

See page 43 in this Instructor's Manual for the handout that accompanies Chapter 14 Computerized Proofreading Application, Job 5, which appears on the template CD-ROM. The solution for this application appears on page 53 of this Instructor's Manual.

CHAPTER 15: Editing for Clarity

TRANSPARENCY MASTERS

Use Transparency Masters 15-1 and 15-2 to demonstrate how to edit for clarity. Use the transparency masters as you did in Chapters 13 and 14, showing the transparencies and discussing how to improve the writing through editing. You also could distribute copies of the masters for extra practice either individually or in groups.

CLASSROOM STRATEGIES AND LEARNING ACTIVITIES

Chapter 15 is the final chapter on editing. This chapter discusses how proofreaders can make communications clear by choosing words carefully and writing with parallel constructions.

Misplaced and Dangling Modifiers

Have students write sentences with misplaced or dangling modifiers for other students to correct. Extra practice with this concept will be time well spent because misplaced and dangling modifiers are sometimes difficult for students to detect.

Parallel Construction

Use an exercise to practice parallel construction where students have to change the wording of text from one parallel style to another parallel style. You can begin this exercise with the following example (parallel text is underscored):

Verbs	My homework includes <u>reading</u> for history, <u>working</u> problems for math, and <u>practicing</u> proofreading.
Nouns	My homework includes history <u>readings</u>, math <u>problems</u>, and proofreading <u>exercises</u>.

LEARNING OBJECTIVES

- Identify misplaced and dangling modifiers.
- Identify errors caused by lack of parallel construction.
- Use simple rather than less familiar words.
- Use strong verbs instead of noun phrases.
- Use appropriate proofreading symbols to indicate changes in text.
- Spell correctly a list of commonly misspelled words.

Simple Words

The emphasis in this section is to use simple words. However, sometimes a less familiar word is the best choice because no other word matches its meaning or a certain word is needed for emphasis. Discuss the writer's role and the proofreader's role in business communications and the importance of choosing the right words and phrases to make messages clear.

Strong Verbs

In the job world, students will encounter writing that uses wordy verb and noun phrase combinations, as many writers use this style. Discuss the readability of messages that are written in a more efficient style.

Spelling Applications

Ten frequently misspelled words are presented. Remind students to look for these words in the chapter proofreading exercises.

COMPUTERIZED PROOFREADING ACTIVITIES

Job 4 is a letter to a customer with whom the writer is on a first-name basis. This letter is written using the individual's first name in the salutation. Students need to proofread and format the letter using the address and other factual information from the source document provided.

Job 5 is a memo to the administrative assistants regarding work assignments. The handwritten notes on the bottom of the handout are Sylvia Guzman's thoughts about the work assignments; she prepared the memo from her notes. Students can refer to the organizational chart for the spellings of names and job titles.

See page 45 in this Instructor's Manual for the handout that accompanies Chapter 15 Computerized Proofreading Application, Job 5, which appears on the template CD-ROM. The solution for this application appears on page 54 of this Instructor's Manual.

TEMPLATE CD ACTIVITIES AND SOLUTIONS

CHAPTER 2: COMPUTERIZED PROOFREADING

Job 5 Proofread and edit a brochure.

1. Proofread the rough draft of the financial services brochure below, and correct any additional errors that you find.

2. Load the file C02JOB5 from the template CD-ROM.

3. Revise the brochure on the CD-ROM according to the rough draft. Make all needed corrections. Spell check the document.

4. Save the page as C02JOB5R.

5. Print the page.

6. Proofread the printed document. If you find additional mistakes, revise, save, and reprint the page.

It is important for all ~~people~~ investors to understand some basic investment terminology to get started with and investment plan. Generally, a retirement savings plan offers several investment options. Typically, these investments fall into three basic groups: equity (stocks), fixed-income (bonds), and short-term investments. There are many names given to the ~~the~~ various investment options for retirement savings plans. We've listed some examples of each below.

Check the investment information provided by your plan to find out the specific investments you are offered.

Equity: Company Stock, Equity Funds, Stock Funds, Growth Funds, Growth and Income Funds, Aggressive Funds, Index Stock Funds

Fixed-Income: Fixed-Income Funds, Bond Funds, U.S. Government Bond Funds, Corporate Bone Funds, Mortgage-Backed Funds, Guaranteed Invesment Contract Funds, Income Funds

Short-Term Investments: Money Market Funds, Cash Management Funds, Reserve Funds, Certificates of Deposit, U.S. Treasury Bill Funds, Short-Term Bond Funds, Short-Term Government Funds

Minneapolis Financial Corp.
928 Irving Avenue S
Minneapolis, MN 55403-7640
Phone (800) 555-0100
Fax (612) 555-0101
minneapolisfinancial.com

CHAPTER 3: COMPUTERIZED PROOFREADING

Job 5 Proofread and edit an electronic letter of inquiry.

1. At the bottom of this page are handwritten notes made by a school administrator. A number of her teachers want to attend software training programs. The teachers have given the administrator their preferences for classes and sessions. Review the notes.

2. Load the file C03JOB5 from the template CD-ROM.

3. On the CD-ROM revise the letter of inquiry that the administrator sent by e-mail. Make sure that its details match the handwritten notes below. Make all needed corrections. In particular, look for the correct use of abbreviations. Spell check the document.

4. Save the file as C03JOB5R.

5. Print the page.

6. Proofread the printed document. If you find additional mistakes, revise, save, and reprint the file.

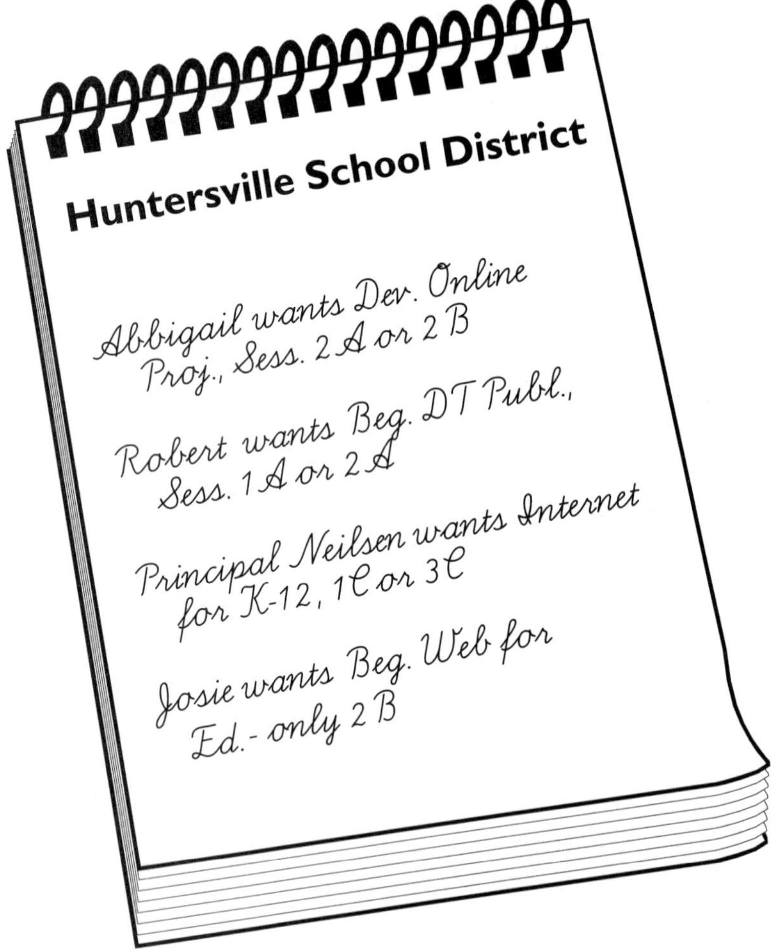

CHAPTER 4: COMPUTERIZED PROOFREADING

Job 6 Proofread and edit a charity auction list.

1. The Partners' Auction date is approaching, and the final list of items to be auctioned is being prepared. Below is a handwritten list of some of the auction items. The list will then be keyed and distributed to the media as well as to auction attendees and television viewers.

2. Load the file C04JOB6 from the template CD-ROM.

3. Proofread the list on the CD-ROM against the handwritten list shown below. Watch for errors in the draft as well as errors that may have been introduced by the person who keyed the list.

4. Save the file as C04JOB6R.

5. Print the list.

6. Proofread the printed document. If you find additional mistakes, revise, save, and reprint the list.

Partners' Auction
February 5, 20--
Auction Board A

Item Number	Item Description and Donor	Retail Value
A748	Dinner for two, Maxwell's (Main Street location)	$50
A749	36 holes of golf, incl. cart rental, Freedom Hills Golf Club	$80
A750	One-day spa visit, including facial, massage, and makeover, Aaah! Spa	$175
A751	Barbecue for ten, Outdoor Entertainments Co.	$280
A752	Movie passes for four, Spring Street Theater	$44
A753	Catered children's party, including games, prizes, and entertainment, Clowns Galore	$110
A754	Four new high-quality tires, including installation, Grand Avenue Tires	$340
A755	One month's supply of fresh coffee beans, The Bean Brewery	$48
A756	Football jersey autographed by John Elway, John Elway	???

CHAPTER 5: COMPUTERIZED PROOFREADING

Job 6   Proofread an e-mail message.

1. Aaron and Gwen Panchuli have found the perfect house, with the help of Terry Andrus at Phelps Real Estate. The Panchulis have applied for and received a home loan and are almost ready to close on their house. Their loan is from Midstate Home Mortgage Co.

2. Load the file C05JOB6 from the template CD-ROM.

3. Proofread the e-mail message on the CD-ROM against the information sheet shown below. The information sheet is correct. In the e-mail, proofread for errors in spelling, abbreviation, word division, and number expression.

4. Save the file as C05JOB6R.

5. Print the e-mail message. Then proofread the printed document. If you find additional mistakes, revise, save, and reprint the e-mail.

CLIENT INFORMATION SHEET

Borrower(s): Aaron H. Panchuli, Gwen D. Panchuli
Address: 3631 Forest Manor
             Indianapolis, IN 46218
Date: 6/30/--

The following is a breakdown of your payment:

Principal and Interest	$ 970.99
Property Taxes	$ 192.77
Hazard Insurance	$ 25.17
Private Mortgage Insurance	$ 67.07
Total Monthly Payment	$ 1,256.00

Your first regular payment is due: August 1

Okja Henning, Mortgage Loan Officer

CHAPTER 6: COMPUTERIZED PROOFREADING

Job 6   Proofread a business letter.

1. After meeting with a client, Emily Smucker has made some notes and drafted a letter. She has transmitted the letter to you by computer—in block style with open punctuation—to proofread and finalize. She has also dropped her notes on your desk so you can double-check the facts and figures. Emily's notes appear below.

2. Load the file C06JOB6 from the template CD-ROM.

3. Proofread the letter on the CD-ROM. Check the letter against Emily's notes to make sure she entered the information correctly. In the letter, watch for errors in spelling, abbreviation, word division, number expression, and format. Spell check the letter.

4. Save the file as C06JOB6R.

5. Print the letter. Then proofread the printed document. If you find additional mistakes, revise, save, and reprint the letter.

CHAPTER 7: COMPUTERIZED PROOFREADING

Job 5 Proofread a memo.

1. Don Jenkins jotted down some notes while reading an article about the convention in Des Moines. Then he drafted a memo for all Chamber staff.

2. Load the file C07JOB5 from the template CD-ROM.

3. Proofread Don's draft, comparing it to the notes he took from the article. The notes are brief but accurate.

4. Finish formatting the memo.

5. Save the file as C07JOB5R.

6. Produce the document by following the standard procedures.

> *convention dates—August 20-25 (Sun.-Fri.)*
> *convention hotel—downtown Ramada Des Moines*
> *Plaza and Palmer are right close by*
> *hotel reservations due by June 21*
> *Clyde/Mae—panel session is Monday at 3:00—everyone should be there*
> *opening session is at dinner on Sun.*
> *Louisville meeting, maybe breakfast, to touch base with Chamber*
> *members—Wednesday*

Job 5 Proofread a personal business letter.

1. Greg Washington, who is interested in attending summer school, has written to Dr. Rosemary Schindler about a special summer program. Greg needs to take a certain number of credit hours to be readmitted to the college as a degree-seeking student. The letter with Mr. Wrenn's instructions is below.

2. Load the file C08JOB5 from the template CD-ROM.

3. Proofread Greg's letter to Dr. Schindler. Check Greg's information against his letter from Mr. Wrenn. Proofread for all errors.

4. Finish formatting the letter using block style with open punctuation.

5. Save the file as C08JOB5R.

6. Produce the document by following the standard procedures.

January 10, 20--

Mr. Greg Washington
4572 East Ninth Street
Chesapeake, VA 23320-4572

Dear Mr. Washington

Your request for readmission to Virginia State College as a psychology major has been reviewed by members of the Admissions Committee and me at our January 8 meeting.

After the third semester a student must have earned 36 hours, and he or she must have a grade point average (GPA) of 1.80 to remain in school.

You were enrolled for three semesters two years ago. During that time you earned 27 hours with a GPA of 1.67. Consequently, readmission is not possible at this time.

We recommend that you attend summer school as a nonmatriculated student. If you do so, you must take two 3-hour courses that are relevant to your major area of study. If you receive a grade of C or better in each of these courses, the committee and I will be happy to reconsider your petition for readmission as a psychology major.

Sincerely yours

Douglas W. Wrenn
Associate Dean

rv

CHAPTER 9: COMPUTERIZED PROOFREADING

Job 5 Proofread advertising copy.

1. Marcos Ortez is preparing a flyer for the Cheney property in Newton Township.

2. Load the file C09JOB5 from the template CD-ROM.

3. Proofread the ad copy on the flyer against the information sheet shown here. The information sheet is correct.

4. Save the file as C09JOB5R.

5. Produce the document by following the standard procedures.

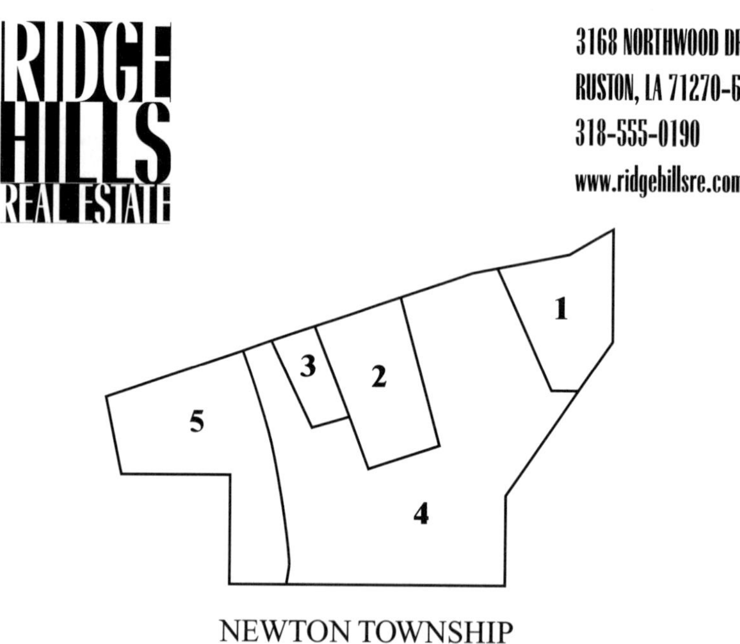

NEWTON TOWNSHIP
CHENEY FARM

LOT		ACRES	PRICE
1	(hilly and wooded)	6.122	$48,900
2	(rolling, partly wooded)	4.504	$39,000
3	(3 BR house and garage)	2.020	$132,500
4	(older barn)	25.296	$79,900
5	(wooded)	13.104	$57,000

Directions
• Take Rt. 13 north to Louisville Rd.
• Turn right; go two miles to County 202. Turn right.
• Go 3.5 miles. Property is on left. Watch for signs.

CHAPTER 10: COMPUTERIZED PROOFREADING

Job 6 Proofread advertising copy.

1. Load the file C10JOB6 from the template CD-ROM.

2. Proofread the advertising copy, and make all necessary corrections. A handwritten draft of the ad copy appears below. Compare the handwritten version with the text in the file.

3. Double-space the text in the document. Use 1″ side margins and a 1 1/2″ top margin. Divide the heading into two lines, double-spacing it. Format the heading in all caps and bold, and quadruple-space after it.

4. Save the document as C10JOB6R.

5. Produce the document by following the standard procedures.

Celebrate the 4th of July at Sahara Resort – We'll give you the works!

A picnic in the park, a swim in the lake, rousing music topped off by fireworks and laser shows that light up an almost perfect starry night! What a better way to show your spirit, then with a 4th of July celebration bursting with color and excitement at Sahara Resort.

After a satisfying day of family fun, lie back and enjoy music by The Deltas. After you watch the Flying High Circus, the celebration will come to a blazing close with a laser show and fireworks display rated to among "the Best in FL." For a real All-American Fourth of July celebration, the place to be is Sahara Resort.

For more information or reservations, contact the Mercado Travel Agency toll free: 1-800-555-0113.

CHAPTER 11: COMPUTERIZED PROOFREADING

Job 5 Proofread a press release.

1. Load the file C11JOB5 from the template CD-ROM.

2. Proofread the press release that Charles Tamara wrote to publicize the next edition of the annual travel guide. Below are the notes he used as he drafted the press release.

3. Format the press release by double-spacing the text, then widening the side margins so that the text fits nicely and looks attractive on two pages. Use 1″ top and bottom margins. Quadruple-space after the heading, and include the page number as a heading on the second page.

4. Save the page as C11JOB5R.

5. Produce the press release by following the standard procedures.

new organization--6 parts

    Appalachian Plateau

    Appalachian Ridge and Valley Reg.

    Blue Ridge

    Piedmont

    Atlantic Coastal plain

    East Gulf Coastal plain

special sections

    day trips

    historical Georgia

    natural Georgia

format

    photography, photography, photography

campaign

    new format

    new information for everyone—not just tourists

CHAPTER 12: COMPUTERIZED PROOFREADING

Job 6 Proofread a memorandum.

1. Sameera Dharia has written a draft of a memo on the bus on the way to work. Once she gets to work, she keys from her draft.

2. Load the file C12JOB6 from the template CD-ROM.

3. Proofread Ms. Dharia's memo, checking it against her handwritten draft. Proofread for errors in keyboarding, abbreviations, number expressions, format, grammar, punctuation, and capitalization.

4. Correctly format the memo using 1″ margins.

5. Save the file as C12JOB6R.

6. Produce the document by following the standard procedures.

To maintain our list of diverse and engaging courses, we must recruit new instructors and test new programming ideas. All proposals for next Fall's classes must be on my desk by 4/1. Following are some guidelines to help you generate ideas.

In addition to our regular 8-wk. course offerings, ~~stay open to~~ consider other formats, such as:

    one-day seminars

    2- or 3-week short courses

    off-site courses (at the art museum? the zoo? the historical society?)

day trips (by coach? by rented van?) →

When you submit a proposal, I need ~~just~~ a few basic pieces of information: Proposed course name, length or duration, potential instructor's name and phone number, an estimated fee, and a brief description. Here's an example:

    Course name: Bonsai   8 2-hour sessions

    Instructor: Ms. Melody Henning, 415-555-0167

    Fee/supplies: $25, plus participants must have a Bonsai Tree

    Description: The course would start with the history of bonsai and its place in Eastern culture. Participants would receive instruction on how to purchase, train, and prune their own plants as well as other varieties ~~as well~~. One or two class sessions would take place at the University's Horticulture Center, where participants would view and study a fascinating variety of bonsai specimens.

Let me emphasize that when you make a proposal, you need not have a commitment from an instructor. These are proposals, not finished plans. I am insistant, though, that your proposals include the length or duration of the course. That information—as much as the description—gives me a sense of the nature of the course.

My gratitude goes to all of you for your hard work and dedication to DHSCC.

CHAPTER 13: COMPUTERIZED PROOFREADING

Job 5 Proofread a business letter.

1. Mazie Dunstan, of TOPS, has written a letter to Mr. Penha Pattison, the manager of B&B Supply Company. She drafted the letter this morning while her computer was being upgraded. After lunch she input the letter. Load the file C13JOB5 from the template CD-ROM.

2. Proofread the letter, and make all necessary corrections. Compare Mrs. Dunstan's handwritten version with the text in the file.

3. Format the letter.

4. Save the document as C13JOB5R.

5. Produce the document by following the standard procedures.

9/28/--

the TOPS office in

I understand there was some confusion about several orders from ~~our~~ Seattle ~~branch~~. In this letter I refer specifically to Order No. LA19284, dated August 21. Let me clarify the situation so that we can continue to do business w/ B&B efficently.

Please be aware that TOPS has three branches in the Seattle area, one in Seattle, one in Tacoma, and one in Auburn. Each office has its own account w/ B&B. Whenever someone from TOPS places an order your staff must verify the office location. In this case the above-referenced order was placed by Rosie Vizquel in Seattle. Tho she gave the Seattle address, apparently it did not register with your database. The Tacoma address got printed on the shipping label, and the arrival of the supplies caused some confusion until several phone calls revealed the nature of the mistake. As a result, there were extra shipping charges (for which you have already indicated you will reimburse us). In addition, the employees in Seattle were in immediate need of some of the supplies.

Rosie Vizquel informs me that three other shipments have been misdirected in the last 9 mos. I know that you will make the necessary changes in your ~~staff's~~ procedures so this won't happen again.

We appreciate the products and services B&B provides, and we look forward to continuing our patronage.

"

CHAPTER 14: COMPUTERIZED PROOFREADING

Job 5 Proofread a business letter.

1. Ada Carlton of Richards & Armon has written a letter to Eve Blosser, who applied for an administrative assistant position with the firm. Miss Carlton wants you to create a response letter using the paragraphs from the form letter (Job 1), encouraging the applicant to further her education and experience. Load the file C14JOB5 from the template CD-ROM.

2. Proofread the letter, and make all necessary corrections. Include Miss Carlton's comments from the draft version below.

3. Format the letter.

4. Save the document as C14JOB5R.

5. Produce the document by following the standard procedures.

[insert date]

May 28

[insert applicant's name and address]

Thank you for your interest in a position at Richards & Armon.

[paragraph A]
We have reviewed your résumé and are impressed with your credentials. Although you are well qualified for an administrative assistant position with our firm, we are completely staffed. We will keep your application in our current files for the next three months. If a position opens within that time, we will contact you to arrange an interview. If you do not hear from us, you may apply with us again after the three-month period.

[paragraph B]
We have reviewed your résumé and note that while you have [insert number of years] years *7* of [insert specific type of experience or just say "office"] experience, you lack training or *including transcription,* education specific to a legal office. We highly recommend the legal office training program at the Houston School of Technology (HST). HST offers day and evening classes in legal terminology, transcription, and legal office technology. The legal office program at HST also coordinates internships for its students so they can begin working in a legal office and gain valuable experience. In fact, we have hired HST internship students. Obtaining this type of specific education and training would help you begin your career in a legal office.

We wish you success in your job search and career.

ADA CARLTON, PERSONNEL MANAGER

lw

(continued on next page)

EVE BLOSSER
1400 South Bennett, Apartment 6
Houston, Texas 77022
(832)555-0178

WORK EXPERIENCE

Receptionist   May 1999 – present
Ballard & May, Certified Public Accountants
Houston, Texas
Answer phones; greet clients; oversee alphabetic filing system; prepare letters and memos from transcription and written drafts

File Clerk   January 1995 – May 1999
Houston Public Schools
Houston, Texas
Oversaw alphabetic and numeric filing systems; worked on Houston Public Schools' central database

Receptionist   June 1993 – December 1994
Conrad Kelly & Associates Real Estate
Houston, Texas
Answered phones; greeted customers and clients

SUMMARY OF QUALIFICATIONS

Regents Business School, Technical Certificate, May 1993
Experienced computer user (word processing, database, and e-mail software)
Excellent communication skills
Strong interpersonal skills
Keyboarding at 90 wpm

CHAPTER 15: COMPUTERIZED PROOFREADING

Job 5 Proofread a memo.

1. Sylvia Guzman has written a memo to the administrative assistants who work at the main offices of Best Natural Products Co. regarding the distribution of work. Load the file C15JOB5 from the template CD-ROM.

2. Proofread the memo, and make any necessary corrections. Consult Ms. Guzman's handwritten notes below. Verify the information against the organizational chart on the next page.

3. Format the memo.

4. Save the document as C15JOB5R.

5. Produce the memo by following the standard procedures.

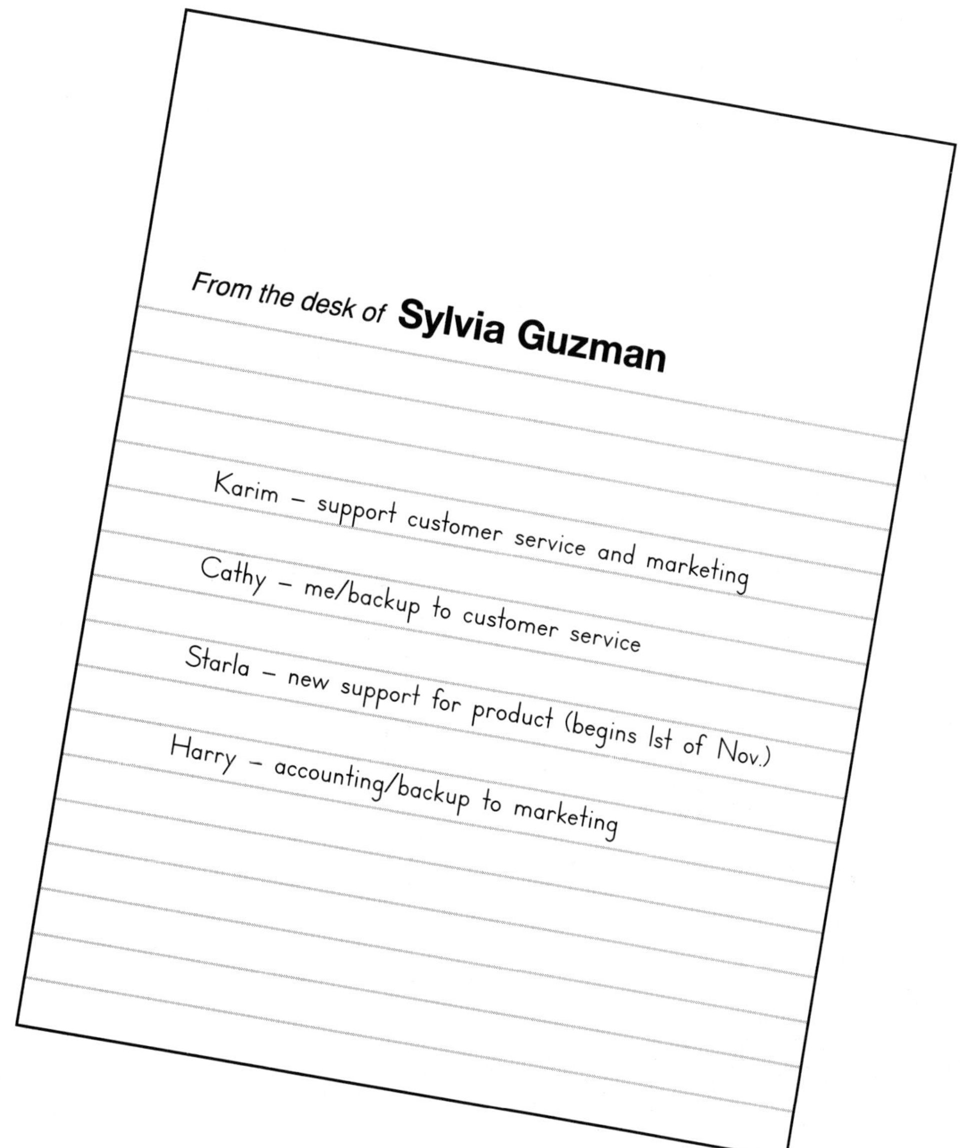

(continued on next page)

Best Natural Products Co.

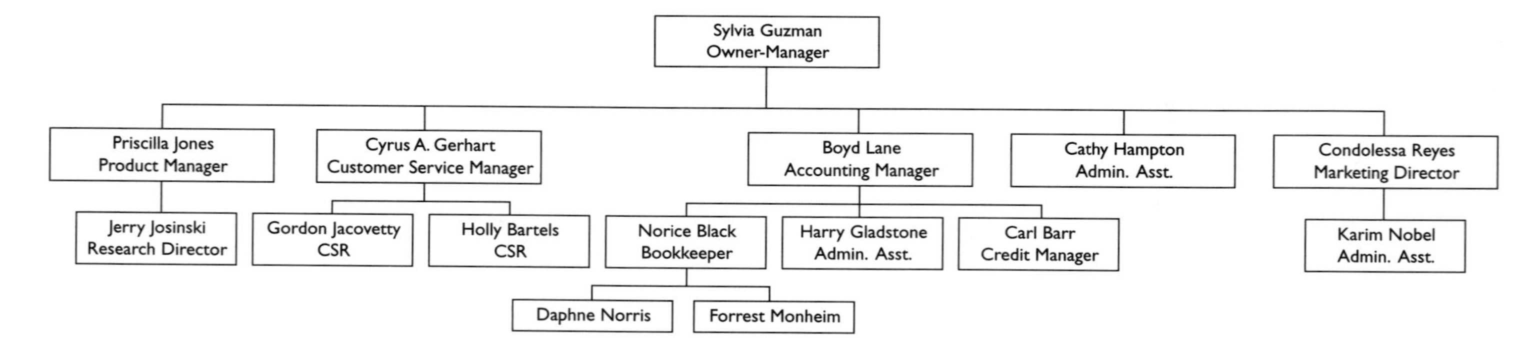

It is important for all investors to understand some basic investment terminology to get started with an investment plan. Generally, a retirement savings plan offers several investment options. Typically, these investments fall into three basic groups: equity (stocks), fixed-income (bonds), and short-term investments. There are many names given to the various investment options for retirement savings plans. We've listed some examples of each below.

Equity: Company Stock, Equity Funds, Stock Funds, Growth Funds, Growth and Income Funds, Aggressive Funds, Index Stock Funds

Fixed-Income: Fixed-Income Funds, Bond Funds, U.S. Government Bond Funds, Corporate Bond Funds, Mortgage-Backed Funds, Guaranteed Investment Contract Funds, Income Funds

Short-Term Investments: Money Market Funds, Cash Management Funds, Reserve Funds, Certificates of Deposit, U.S. Treasury Bill Funds, Short-Term Bond Funds, Short-Term Government Funds

Check the investment information provided by your plan to find out the specific investments you are offered.

Date: Tuesday, 24 April 20-- 13:53:16
From: L Bargender <Lbargender@hsd.k12.edu>
To: Garry Morrison <Morrison@SSLC.com>
Subject: Re: Registration for Summer Sessions

Mr. Morrison

As I indicated in our telephone conversation on Wednesday, April 18, four teachers from Huntersville School District (HSD) wish to attend classes this summer at Software Success Learning Center. Their names, street addresses, and the classes for which they wish to register appear below. Class sessions are listed in order of preference.

Abbigail Waters
1227 Patman Avenue
Cornelius, NC 28031

Development of Online Projects for Secondary Students, Session 2A or 2B

Robert Novello
414 Beach Lane
Mooresville, NC 28117

Beginning Desktop Publishing for Educators, Session 1A or 2A
Fundamentals of Classroom Technology, Session 1B

Dr. Al Neilsen
14277 Shepherds Court
Huntersville, NC 28078

The Internet for K-12 Educators, Session 1C or 3C

Josie DiCarlo
6446 Winding Ridge Road
Huntersville, NC 28078

Beginning Web Pages for Educators, Session 2B

The teachers have several queries. If you e-mail your responses to me, I will forward them to the appropriate teachers.

Mr. Novello needs information about the wheelchair accessibility of the building, including access from the parking lot.

Mrs. DiCarlo has a conflict with one of the class sessions. Will she be able to make up or somehow cover the material she misses?

Please send billing information to my attention at the address below. Please note that the teachers need confirmation of registration before the school year ends on Wednesday, June 9.

The HSD teachers who attended last summer's classes regarded the program as 100 percent effective. On behalf of our students, thank you.

Linda Bargender, Senior Administrator
Huntersville School District
109 Huntersville-Concord Road
Huntersville, NC 28078

Partners' Auction
February 5, 20--
Auction Board A

Item Number	Item Description and Donor	Retail Value
A748	Dinner for two, Maxwell's (Main Street location)	$50
A749	36 holes of golf, including cart rental, Freedom Hills Golf Club	$80
A750	One-day spa visit, including facial, massage, and makeover, Aaah! Spa	$175
A751	Barbecue for ten, Outdoor Entertain-ments Co.	$280
A752	Movie passes for four, Spring Street Theater	$44
A753	Catered children's party, including games, prizes, and entertainment, Clowns Galore	$110
A754	Four new high-quality tires, including installation, Grand Avenue Tires	$340
A755	One month's supply of fresh coffee beans, The Bean Brewery	$48
A756	Football jersey autographed by John Elway, John Elway	???

Return-Path: OHenning@midstate.com

From: OHenning@midstate.com

Date: Wed, 28 June 20-- 08:43:06 EDT

Subject: RE: Payment Information

To: panchuli@echonet.net

Aaron and Gwen,

You must be excited about your closing on Friday. I will meet you at the title office on East 79th Street just before the 10 a.m. meeting.

I know you were eager to see the breakdown of your future mortgage payments. On Friday I will give you an information sheet for your files. In the meantime, here is a breakdown for you.

The principal and interest portion of your payment is $970.99. Property taxes add another $192.77. The hazard insurance is $25.17, and the private mortgage insurance is $67.07. That comes to a total monthly payment of $1,256.

Your first payment is due on August 1. I can answer any questions you may have when I see you on Friday.

In the meantime, congratulations on your first house!

Okja Henning
Mortgage Loan Officer
Midstate Home Mortgage Co.
3810 East 81st Street
Indianapolis, IN 46240-1411
(317) 555-0187

March 18, 20—

Ms. Joanna Leasburg
Vice President, Operations
ILD Computer Systems, Inc.
3810 Peachtree Road NE
Atlanta, GA 30319-3303

Dear Ms. Leasburg

It was a pleasure to meet with you yesterday. Our meeting was a productive one, and it gives us a good start on your project. Following are my initial thoughts about the current state of ILD's work spaces and about improvements that you could make to the work environment.

The cubicles in the main work area are of standard dimensions--10 feet by 10 feet. However, the cubicle walls are shorter than is recommended. To maximize privacy, cubicle walls should be at least 5 feet high, and many experts recommend that walls be 6 feet high. I recommend that you replace the existing 4-foot-high cubicles. New cubicle partitions with special acoustic properties would decrease the noise level. Also, the layout could be altered so that cubicle entrances are staggered. Workers are distracted when they can see into another cubicle.

Within the existing cubicles the computers are positioned so that workers' backs are toward the cubicle entrance. This creates a potential privacy or security risk in that someone could read the computer screen from behind a worker without that worker's knowledge. A more efficient setup would be to position each worker so that his or her side is toward the entrance. This would allow the worker to be more aware of people who enter the cubicle or who require his or her attention from the entrance.

I will consult my colleague, Pamela DeVore, on the lighting. With her expertise we can remedy the inadequate ambient lighting so that workers need not rely on task lighting. Pamela will issue a separate letter with her evaluation.

As we discussed, these initial comments are meant to spur discussions among management and staff at ILD. Let's reserve March 30 for our next meeting. After you receive feedback from your colleagues, we will take the next step toward making ILD Computer Systems a more comfortable and productive place to work.

Cordially

Ms. Emily E. Smucker
Regional Manager

ri

TO: All Chamber Staff

FROM: Don Jenkins

DATE: June 10, 20--

SUBJECT: U.S. CHAMBER OF COMMERCE CONVENTION

Here are some reminders about the upcoming convention.

The convention runs an extra day this year—from Sunday through Friday, August 20-25. The opening session is a banquet on Sunday evening starting at 6 p.m., so plan sufficient time for traveling earlier in the day.

The convention is being held at the downtown Ramada Des Moines; the Plaza and Palmer Hotels are nearby. Plenty of restaurants are in the area as well. Each of you is responsible for making your own hotel arrangements. The deadline is June 21.

Plan to attend the session titled "Fostering Businesses Owned by Women and Minorities" on Monday afternoon at three. Clyde and our former economic director, Mae Liebert, are serving on the panel that will discuss the importance of women and minorities in our business communities.

Finally, please reserve two hours on Wednesday morning for breakfast at the Ramada with all of the attending Louisville Chamber members. The Convention Housing Bureau is helping us make these arrangements. Alexis and I are planning an article for the July newsletter to inform our members about the convention.

Our presence at this convention gives our members confidence in our ability to continue to lead Louisville into the twenty-first century. Every one of us is fortunate to represent Louisville. Let's make sure our members know that too.

Mr. Greg Washington
4572 East Ninth Street
Chesapeake, VA 23320-4572
February 9, 20--

Dr. Rosemary Schindler
Director of Academic Development
Virginia State College
989 Johnstown Road
Chesapeake, VA 23320-4961

Dear Dr. Schindler

I wish to re-enroll in Virginia State College as a full-time student. I was enrolled two years ago but left after three semesters for personal reasons. I have been instructed by Mr. Wrenn to attend summer school. He told me to accumulate some credit hours and increase my grade point average so that I can apply for readmission.

As a result of his instructions, I have reviewed the summer course offerings in psychology, my major area of study. Though many courses are offered, none of them meets my particular interests. I spoke to Mrs. Tiberi, one of my former instructors. I proposed to her a directed study in child psychology at the day care where I am working this summer. She said she would be willing to oversee such a project, if it were approved by you.

I would be more than happy to work with Mrs. Tiberi to develop a course outline, course objectives, or whatever other documentation you need. Because I am willing to devote all of my time to this project, I am hoping that this one course would be worth six credit hours. I need at least that much to be able to apply for readmission in the fall.

I appreciate your considering my proposal, Dr. Schindler. You may speak to Mrs. Tiberi or me about my ideas. You can reach me at home, 555-0112. I understand the deadline for getting approval of special summer programs is May 14. I look forward to hearing from you.

Sincerely

Greg Washington

ARE YOU ALL READY TO LIVE IN THE COUNTRY?

If you're ready for less stress, less traffic, and fewer headaches, Ridge Hills Real Estate has found the place for you. Beautiful, rolling land that is a mix of meadow and woods awaits you just a short drive past Newton Township. Would you like to see it? Take your camera! From Ruston go north on Route 13 to Louisville Road. Turn right and go 2 miles to County 202. Turn right and go 3.5 miles. The property is on the left. Watch for signs. Once you experience this land, we think you'll want to call us.

Asad Roberts	318-555-0190, Ext. 114
Carla Hodge	318-555-0190, Ext. 117
Maribel Landaverde	318-555-0190, Ext. 131

Lot 1: 6.122 acres of hilly and wooded land. Several picture-perfect home sites among the trees. $48,900

Lot 2: Partly wooded and rolling, 4.504 acres. Build a house well back from the road, and see nothing but sky and trees out your windows. $39,000

Lot 3: 2.02 acres and the house is already built! The 3-bedroom older farmhouse needs your TLC, but wait until you see the view from the porch. A lawn of rolling green hills lies between the porch and the pond, which is the perfect complement for a country home. $132,500

Lot 4: These 25.296 acres could be yours. An older but sturdy barn on the property implies that you could house horses, llamas, or goats if you so choose. Or perhaps you could just enjoy the quiet setting, as you have always dreamed of doing. $79,900

Lot 5: A wooded 13.104-acre site that could be your year-round sanctuary. Enjoy an abundance of wildlife every day. $57,000

CELEBRATE THE FOURTH OF JULY AT SAHARA RESORT

WE'LL GIVE YOU THE WORKS!

A picnic in the park, a swim in the lake, rousing music topped off by fireworks and laser shows that light up an almost perfect starry night. What better way to show your spirit than with a Fourth of July celebration bursting with color and excitement at Sahara Resort.

After a satisfying day of family fun, lie back and enjoy music by The Deltas. After you watch the Flying High Circus, the celebration will come to a blazing close with a laser show and fireworks display rated to be among "the Best in Florida." For a real All-American Fourth of July celebration, the place to be is Sahara Resort.

For more information or reservations, contact the Mercado Travel Agency toll free, 1-800-555-0113.

PRESS RELEASE

August 8, 20--

Georgia's Department of Tourism is changing the format of its Annual Travel Guide significantly this year; a statewide survey had shown that users wanted to see a more updated publication. Following is a summary of the changes. The guide, titled *Georgia—A Peach of a State,* is published annually and is available starting in November for the following calendar year. *Georgia—A Peach of a State* is undoubtedly a valuable part of Georgia's tourism industry.

Overall Organization

Instead of a county-by-county format (as in the past), the guide is organized by region. The regions are as follows: (1) the Appalachian Plateau, (2) the Appalachian Ridge and Valley Region, (3) the Blue Ridge, (4) the Piedmont, (5) the Atlantic Coastal Plain, and (6) the East Gulf Coastal Plain. So the six main sections of the book are ordered and titled as presented here. Each section—as users would expect—includes a detailed map of the region.

Special-Interest Sections

There are also a number of large sections that help travelers with special interests. One chapter, titled "Day Trips," outlines a number of one-day automobile trips from each of the state's ten major metropolitan areas. The chapter titled "Historical Georgia" highlights special places to visit, such as Historic Savannah, the Dahlonega Gold Museum, the Antebellum Trail, the Etowah Mounds, and the Atlanta History Center. Finally, a chapter titled "Natural Georgia" focuses on the state's national and state parklands as well as its 79 wildlife management areas.

Visual Impact

Analysis of last year's user survey indicated that the guide was lacking in photographs. For that reason the upcoming guide will be brimming with color

2

photographs of our beautiful state. The Department of Tourism expects the pictures to speak for themselves—after all, it's Georgia's beauty that brings people here in the first place.

Using the Guide

This year's marketing campaign will capitalize on the updated format. Even long-time Georgia residents will find something new and interesting in the updated guide.

The guide isn't just for tourists—it's for anyone who lives in, drives in, or loves Georgia.

TO: DHSCC Programming Staff

FROM :   Sameera Dharia

DATE: January 11, 20--

SUBJECT: PROGRAMMING PROPOSALS

To maintain our list of diverse and engaging courses, we must recruit new instructors and test new programming ideas. All proposals for next fall's classes must be on my desk by April 1. Following are some guidelines to help you generate ideas.

In addition to our regular eight-week course offerings, consider other formats, such as these:
- One-day seminars
- Two- or three-week short courses
- Off-site courses (at the art museum? the zoo? the historical society?)
- Day trips (by coach? by rented van?)

When you submit a proposal, I need a few basic pieces of information: proposed course name, length or duration, potential instructor's name and phone number, an estimated fee, and a brief description. Here's an example:

Course name: Bonsai   8 two-hour sessions
Instructor: Ms. Melody Henning, 415-555-0167
Fee/supplies: $25, plus participants must have a bonsai tree
Description: The course would start with the history of bonsai and its place in Eastern culture. Participants would receive instruction in how to purchase, train, and prune their own plants as well as other varieties. One or two class sessions would take place at the university's Horticulture Center, where participants would view and study a fascinating variety of bonsai specimens.

Let me emphasize that when you make a proposal, you need not have a commitment from an instructor. These are proposals, not finished plans. I am insistent, though, that your proposals include the length or duration of the course. That information—as much as the description— gives me a sense of the nature of the course.

My gratitude goes to all of you for your hard work and dedication to DHSCC.

September 28, 20--

Mr. Penha Pattison, Manager
B&B Supply Company
P.O. Box 5314
Phoenix, AZ 20721-8011

Dear Mr. Pattison

I understand there was some confusion about several orders from the TOPS office in Seattle. In this letter I refer specifically to Order No. LA19284, dated August 21. Let me clarify the situation so that we can continue to do business with B&B efficiently.

Please be aware that TOPS has three branches in the Seattle area—one in Seattle, one in Tacoma, and one in Auburn. Each office has its own account with B&B. Whenever someone from TOPS places an order, your staff must verify the office location. In this case the above-referenced order was placed by Rosie Vizquel in Seattle. Though she gave the Seattle address, apparently it did not register with your database. The Tacoma address got printed on the shipping label, and the arrival of the supplies caused some confusion until several phone calls revealed the nature of the mistake. As a result, there were extra shipping charges (for which you have already indicated you will reimburse us). In addition, the employees in Seattle were in immediate need of some of the supplies.

Rosie Vizquel informs me that three other shipments have been misdirected in the last nine months. I know that you will make the necessary changes in your procedures so this will not happen again.

We appreciate the products and services B&B provides, and we look forward to continuing our patronage.

Cordially

Mazie Dunstan

c Rosie Vizquel

May 28, 20—

Ms. Eve Blosser
1400 South Bennett, Apartment 6
Houston, TX 77022

Thank you for your interest in a position at Richards & Armon.

We have reviewed your résumé and note that while you have [insert the correct number] years of office experience, including transcription, you lack training or education specific to a legal office. We highly recommend the legal office training program at the Houston School of Technology (HST). HST offers day and evening classes in legal terminology, transcription, and legal office technology. The legal office program at HST also coordinates internships for its students so they can begin working in a legal office and gain valuable experience. In fact, we have hired HST internship students. Obtaining this type of specific education and training would help you begin your career in a legal office.

We wish you success in your job search and career.

ADA CARLTON, PERSONNEL MANAGER

lw

TO: Administrative Assistants

FROM: Sylvia Guzman

DATE: October 28, 20—

SUBJECT: Work Assignments

Although I have spoken with each of you individually, I wanted to put in writing the work assignments for the administrative assistants at our home office. Principal assignments will not drastically change; however, two new changes will take effect November 1. First, we hired a new administrative assistant. Starla Jessup will begin her employment with BNPC on November 1. Secondly, we are creating secondary assignments to help balance the workload among the four administrative assistants.

- Cathy will remain my assistant. She will be secondary support for Customer Service.
- Karim will remain the administrative assistant to Marketing. In addition, he will support Customer Service. Karim's role in Customer Service will be a regular assignment, not a secondary support assignment.
- Harry will remain the administrative assistant to Accounting. He will be secondary support for Marketing.
- Starla will support Product/R&D. The product and research people have enough administrative support in the field and at the plants; however, we must now provide administrative support here at the home office.

While we thoroughly appreciate the growth our company is enjoying, the "growing pains" we are experiencing now are reminiscent of when we first started BNPC over 12 years ago. I want to commend your efforts in creating a pleasant, courteous work environment for everyone here. It has been said that administrative support is the backbone of a company. I know that's true for us.

We can discuss these assignments, and I will answer any questions you have at our staff meeting next Wednesday. Working together, we can balance the workload with these new assignments.

TRANSPARENCY MASTERS

TM2-1	Proofreading Symbols—Omissions, Additions, and Misstrokes
TM2-2	Proofreading Symbols—Transposition and Draft Applications
TM2-3	Keyboarding Errors
TM3-1	Proofreading Symbols—Errors in Abbreviations
TM3-2	Abbreviation Exercises
TM3-3	Abbreviation Exercises (continued)
TM3-4	Abbreviation Rules
TM4-1	Word Division Exercises
TM4-2	Word Division Exercises (continued)
TM4-3	Word Division Rules
TM5-1	Number Expression Exercises
TM5-2	Number Expression Exercises (continued)
TM5-3	Number Expression Exercises (continued)
TM5-4	Number Expression Exercises (continued)
TM6-1	Proofreading Symbols—Format Applications
TM6-2	Proofreading Symbols—Format Applications (continued)
TM6-3	Block Letter Style (with open punctuation)
TM6-4	Modified Block Letter Style (with mixed punctuation)
TM6-5	Simplified Letter Style
TM6-6	Memorandum
TM6-7	Unbound Report
TM6-8	Unbound Report (continued)
TM7-1	Parts of a Sentence
TM7-2	Subject-Verb Agreement
TM7-3	Subject-Verb Agreement (continued)
TM7-4	Subject-Verb Agreement (continued)
TM7-5	Subject-Verb Agreement (continued)
TM7-6	Sentence Faults
TM8-1	Pronouns
TM8-2	Pronoun Exercises
TM8-3	Pronoun Exercises (continued)
TM8-4	Pronoun Exercises (continued)
TM8-5	Gender-Neutral Language Exercises
TM9-1	Exercises for Errors in Words Often Confused
TM9-2	Exercises for Errors in Words Often Confused (continued)
TM9-3	Exercises for Errors in Words Often Confused (continued)
TM9-4	Exercises for Errors in Words Often Confused (continued)
TM9-5	Words Deserving Special Consideration
TM10-1	Terminal Punctuation Exercises
TM10-2	Internal Punctuation Exercises
TM10-3	Internal Punctuation Exercises (continued)

TM10-4   Internal Punctuation Exercises (continued)
TM10-5   Internal Punctuation Exercises (continued)
TM10-6   Internal Punctuation Exercises (continued)
TM11-1   Exercises for Semicolons
TM11-2   Exercises for Colons
TM11-3   Exercises for Apostrophes
TM11-4   Exercises for Quotation Marks
TM11-5   Exercises for Underscores and Italics
TM11-6   Exercises for the Dash
TM11-7   Exercises for Parentheses
TM11-8   Exercises for Brackets
TM12-1   Capitalization Exercises
TM12-2   Capitalization Exercises (continued)
TM12-3   Capitalization Exercises (continued)
TM12-4   Capitalization Exercises (continued)
TM12-5   Capitalization Exercises (continued)
TM12-6   Capitalization Exercises (continued)
TM13-1   Editing for Content
TM13-2   Editing for Content (continued)
TM14-1   Editing for Conciseness
TM14-2   Editing for Conciseness (continued)
TM15-1   Editing for Clarity
TM15-2   Editing for Clarity (continued)

PROOFREADING SYMBOLS
Omissions, Additions, and Misstrokes

∧ Insert copy

Send applications to Human Resources by Tuesday, July 16.

Insert space

Department managers must assess each employee's performance.

⊂ Close up space

The company picnic is scheduled for Saturday, July 21.

⟋ Delete copy

No one person is to blame.

∧ Insert character

Please plan a training meeting.

⟋ Delete character

Accuracy is vital on all our documents.

⟋ Delete character; close up space

I hope to have an one-time departure.

/ Change character

The paper is stick in the copier.

PROOFREADING SYMBOLS
Transposition and Draft Applications

⌣	Transpose	The panel has reveiwed your application.
(move copy symbol)	Move copy	The annual sales meeting brings together 324 salespeople in Atlanta.
stet or . . .	Let it stand	Company policy (Sec. 12.8) states that casual day "occurs only on Friday." When Friday is a scheduled holiday, employees may dress casually on ~~Thursday~~ of that *stet* week.
——	Change copy	All employees should submit their paperwork to the ~~Human Resources~~ *Personnel* Department.

KEYBOARDING ERRORS

Check closely for the following kinds of keyboarding errors:

- Omitted letters or characters in words

- Omitted spaces, words, phrases, or lines of text

- Repeated words, especially short words at the beginnings and ends of lines

- Omitted or added single letters, digits, words, or spaces

- Misstrokes, particularly at the ends of words

- Errors involving numerical data

- Sequences of dates and enumerations

- Transposed letters, numbers, words, or sentences

PROOFREADING SYMBOLS
Errors in Abbreviations

Spell out.	We are the biggest producer of recycled plastics in the U.S.
	Our president, Geo. Shimizu, founded the company nine years ago.
Insert a period.	The lecture begins at 7 pm.
	The conference in St Louis was an international gathering of educators.
Delete a period; close up space.	In April the I.R.S. is accessible at all hours.
	The home office is located at 2044 Reed Road, S.E., in Denver.

Answers: Spell out: United States, George; Insert a period: p.m., St. Louis; Delete period; close up space: IRS, SE

ABBREVIATION EXERCISES

3-1   Spell out first names.

> Wm. Carver will retire at the end of May.

3-2   Always abbreviate certain personal titles, and always use a period.

> Mister Richard Han will speak at the luncheon prepared in Doctor Callende's honor.

3-3   Abbreviate agency and organization names by using capital letters that are *not* separated by periods.

> The growing membership of M.A.D.D. is becoming a significant political force.

Spell out *United States* when used as a noun.

> Some school children in the U.S. benefit from subsidized breakfasts.

3-4   Abbreviate time designations.

> The program will be aired at 7:30 p.m. central standard time.

Answers: 3-1: William; 3-2: Mr., Dr.; 3-3: MADD, United States; 3-4: CST

ABBREVIATION EXERCISES
(continued)

3-5   Spell out street addresses. Spell out compass directions before a street name in text and inside addresses.

     1210 Dennison Ave.   372 S. Appleton Rd.

3-6   Spell out units of measure in formal text; otherwise, abbreviated units of measure do not contain periods.

     The 12-mi course has a soft dirt surface.

WHAT TO BRING TO THE PICNIC		
Danny	Patricia	Mary Jo
25 soft drinks, 2 L each	20 yd paper to cover tables	5 packages ground beef, 2 lb each

3-7   Do not use a period after a shortened word form.

     In your memorandum you refer to a facsimile sent from Sean.

3-8   Spell out most symbols in formal text.

     More than 35% of our employees responded to the survey sent out by the accounting & development departments.

Answers: 3-5: Avenue, South, Road; 3-6: 12-mile; 3-7: memo, fax; 3-8: percent, and

ABBREVIATION RULES

Keep in mind the following rules pertaining to abbreviations:

- Spell out personal names in text.

- Abbreviate personal titles such as *Mrs.*

- Do not use periods in agency and organization names whose abbreviations are in all capital letters.

- When abbreviating names of countries, use initials followed by periods.

- Use all capital letters and no periods for time zone abbreviations; designations for morning and afternoon should always appear as *a.m.* and *p.m.*

- Spell out all words in street addresses unless using a format in which space is limited.

- Spell out units of measure and names of symbols, such as *percent,* in formal text.

- Do not use periods with abbreviated units of measure.

WORD DIVISION EXERCISES

4-1 Divide words between syllables.

     garbage   marked   pamphlet

4-2 Leave at least two characters on the upper line and at least three characters on the lower line.

     evokes   extend   roughly

4-3 Divide a compound word between words.

     membership   vice-president   halfback

4-4 Divide a word *after* a single-letter syllable unless that syllable precedes certain endings, such as *-fy, -ble, -bly, -cle, -cal,* and *-ly.*

     document   notify   miracle   affirmative

4-5 Divide a word between two single-vowel syllables.

     notoriety   reconciliation   mediate

4-6 Divide a word after a prefix or before a suffix.

     befriend   internment   stylist

Answers: 4-1: gar- bage, marked, pam- phlet; 4-2: evokes, ex- tend, roughly; 4-3: member- ship, vice- president, half- back; 4-4: docu- ment, not- ify, mir- acle, affirma- tive; 4-5: notori- ety, reconcili-ation, medi- ate; 4-6: be- friend, intern- ment, styl- ist

WORD DIVISION EXERCISES
(continued)

4-7   Divide a word between double consonants unless the word normally ends in double consonants and has a suffix that adds an extra syllable.

    bluffing   mammoth   installed

4-9   Avoid dividing words of fewer than six letters.

    dusty   copy   level   enter

4-10   Do not divide abbreviations, contractions, and numbers.

    NASA   couldn't   Part No. 5293-382

4-11   If necessary, divide a URL after the double slashes or before a dot or the @ sign, but do not add a hyphen.

    http://www.usps.gov   pkale@purdue.edu

4-12   Avoid dividing between word pairs that should be read as a unit.

    April 10, 1986   Miss Alice Tucker   442 Salt Lane

Answers: 4-7: bluff- ing, mam- moth, installed; 4-9: (no divisions); 4-10: (no divisions); 4-11: http:// / www.usps.gov or http://www / .usps.gov, pkale / @purdue.edu; 4-12: April 10, / 1986, Miss Alice / Tucker, 442 Salt / Lane

WORD DIVISION RULES

- Divide a word between syllables.

- Leave at least two characters (plus the hyphen) on the upper line and three characters (which could include punctuation) on the lower line.

- Divide compound words between the words.

- In a word that contains a single-vowel syllable, divide after the single vowel; in a word that contains two single-vowel syllables, divide between those two vowels.

- Usually, divide a word after a prefix or before a suffix.

- Usually, divide a word between double consonants.

- Avoid dividing words of fewer than six letters.

- Do not divide abbreviations, contractions, or most numbers.

NUMBER EXPRESSION EXERCISES

5-1   Use words for numbers 1 through 10; use figures for numbers greater than 10.

> We delivered 4 loads of bark to the park for the fifty-four volunteers who were planting trees.

5-2   Be consistent in a series of related numbers.

> The animal shelter had 18 dogs, seven puppies, twenty-six cats, and 17 kittens.

5-3   Use figures for emphasis.

> The interest rate on our loan is six percent.

Use words in nontechnical text if a number does not need emphasis and can be expressed in one or two words.

> Of the 30 members, only a few disagreed.

5-4   Use figures *and* words for large round numbers.

> We anticipate sales of 17,000,000 units.

5-5   Spell out one- or two-word numbers that begin a sentence.

> 67 employees attended the banquet.

Answers: 5-1: four loads, 54 volunteers; 5-2: 7 puppies, 26 cats; 5-3: 6 percent, thirty members; 5-4: 17 million; 5-5: Sixty-seven

NUMBER EXPRESSION EXERCISES
(continued)

5-6   In two adjacent numbers with one number part of a compound modifier, spell out the number of the smallest word.

   There were 12 four-wheeled carts in the race.

   This envelope needs 1 thirty-four-cent stamp.

5-7   Use words for one- or two-word ordinals.

   The facilitator was late for the 1st meeting.

5-8   Spell out street names from one through ten.

   The office on 4th Avenue is closed.

5-9   Use words for ages ten and under, but use figures for ages expressed in business documents.

   Sheila Burnes, age 32, left the company when she adopted 2-year-old twin boys.

5-10   Use figures to express numbers preceded by nouns.

   In Section two notice Figures five and eleven.

Answers: 5-6: one 34-cent stamp; 5-7: first meeting; 5-8: Fourth Avenue; 5-9: two-year-old; 5-10: Section 2, Figures 5 and 11

NUMBER EXPRESSION EXERCISES
(continued)

5-11 Spell out a simple fraction that stands alone if it is easy to express; use figures for compound fractions.

Nearly 1/3 of the staff is at the conference.

The pipe was two and one-fourth inches too short.

5-12 Use words with *o'clock* or when the hour stands alone. Use figures with *a.m., p.m., noon,* and *midnight.*

The plane arrives around 7 o'clock.

I'll be finished at work by 6.

The meeting was postponed until two p.m.

5-13 In a date use ordinal figures when a day stands alone or precedes the month.

The deadline was the eighteenth, but we didn't finish until the twenty-first of July.

5-14 Express periods of time in figures for emphasis.

The thirty-year mortgage rate is dropping.

5-15 Use figures with units of measure.

The lot measures sixty feet by ninety-eight feet.

Answers: 5-11: one-third, 2 1/4 inches; 5-12: seven o'clock, by six, 2 p.m.; 5-13: 18th, 21st; 5-14: 30-year mortgage; 5-15: 60 feet by 98 feet

NUMBER EXPRESSION EXERCISES
(continued)

5-16 Use figures to express amounts of money.

The seminar fee is forty-five dollars for members.

5-17 Use figures to express percents and decimals.

My account has an APR of nine percent, but her account has an APR of twelve point nine percent.

5-18 Use figures with abbreviations or symbols, and repeat the symbols in a range of numbers for clarity.

seventy-four° No. sixty-two

30-35% $10-20

5-19 Use figures for serial numbers or other long series of numbers.

Cancel Purchase Order No. three five one.

5-20 Telephone/fax numbers are usually divided into area code, first three numbers, and remaining numbers. Use parentheses, hyphens, or periods to separate groups of numbers.

Dial 1-888-NEW-ROOF for a free estimate.

For an application, call 1-800-555-0156.

Answers: 5-16: $45; 5-17: 9 percent, 12.9 percent; 5-18: 74°, 30%-35%, No. 62, $10-$20; 5-19: No. 351; 5-20: C

PROOFREADING SYMBOLS
Format Applications

SS	Single-space.	Dr. Ahmad Priestly SS [3470 35th Street Kenosha, WI 53140
DS	Double-space.	DS [Dear Dr. Priestly: Pro/Office Interiors is the area's one-stop design center.
QS	Quadruple-space.	Sincerely QS [PRO/OFFICE INTERIORS Stephen W. Berg
# No #	Start a new paragraph; do not start a new paragraph.	No further vacation requests will be accepted. # With regard to next week's summer fair, employees may wear office casual attire. No # Office casual attire must adhere to established guidelines.
‖	Align copy.	TO: ‖ Mark Oppenheimer FROM: ‖ Cheryl Wells DATE: ‖ November 8, 20--

TM6-1

PROOFREADING SYMBOLS
Format Applications
(continued)

Symbol	Meaning	Example
/ ≡	Change to lowercase or capital letter.	Mr. Austin McDonald 1203 Highland Street Boise, Id 83704
—	Set underscore or italics.	Other resources. The people you know are invaluable. Let everyone know you are looking for a job.
(delete symbols) No ital	Delete underscore or italics.	Other resources. The people you know are invaluable. Let everyone know you are looking for a job.
][ ] [x|	Center; move left; move right; move a specified amount of space.	Telecommunications Hands-free operation of telecommunications equipment is optimal.
+1ℓ✳︎→ −1ℓ✳︎→	Insert a line; delete a line.	1. Fan the paper. +1ℓ✳︎→ 2. Insert paper into the tray. 3. Close the door, and −1ℓ✳︎→ secure with the lever.

BLOCK LETTER STYLE
(with open punctuation)

P.O. Box 441
Brooklin, ME 04616
207.555.0114
www.markel.com

April 10, 20--

Mr. Mitchell Watanabe
359 Boat Lane
Brooklin, ME 04616

Dear Mr. Watanabe

Enclosed are the pamphlets you requested at the Home and Remodeling Show last week. Markel carries all of the roofing materials described in the literature. If you have any further questions after reading the pamphlets, please feel free to call.

Markel Roofing is a family-owned company that has been in business for 48 years. We treat each house as if it were our own, using quality materials installed by experts. You can use our industry expertise to make informed choices about roofing materials, venting options, and installation methods.

A new roof from Markel will keep your home safe and sound for years and years. You have my word on it—and my father's word and my grandfather's word.

When you are ready for an estimate on your new roof, call me.

Sincerely

Dennis Markel, Owner

fd

Enclosures

MODIFIED BLOCK LETTER STYLE
(with mixed punctuation)

P.O. Box 441
Brooklin, ME 04616
207.555.0114
www.markel.com

April 10, 20--

Mr. Mitchell Watanabe
359 Boat Lane
Brooklin, ME 04616

Dear Mr. Watanabe:

Enclosed are the pamphlets you requested at the Home and Remodeling Show last week. Markel carries all of the roofing materials described in the literature. If you have any further questions after reading the pamphlets, please feel free to call.

Markel Roofing is a family-owned company that has been in business for 48 years. We treat each house as if it were our own, using quality materials installed by experts. You can use our industry expertise to make informed choices about roofing materials, venting options, and installation methods.

A new roof from Markel will keep your home safe and sound for years and years. You have my word on it—and my father's word and my grandfather's word.

When you are ready for an estimate on your new roof, call me.

Sincerely,

Dennis Markel, Owner

fd

Enclosures

SIMPLIFIED LETTER STYLE

P.O. Box 441
Brooklin, ME 04616
207.555.0114
www.markel.com

April 10, 20--

Mr. Mitchell Watanabe
359 Boat Lane
Brooklin, ME 04616

ROOFING INFORMATION

Enclosed are the pamphlets you requested at the Home and Remodeling Show last week. Markel carries all of the roofing materials described in the literature. If you have any further questions after reading the pamphlets, please feel free to call.

Markel Roofing is a family-owned company that has been in business for 48 years. We treat each house as if it were our own, using quality materials installed by experts. You can use our industry expertise to make informed choices about roofing materials, venting options, and installation methods.

A new roof from Markel will keep your home safe and sound for years and years. You have my word on it—and my father's word and my grandfather's word.

When you are ready for an estimate on your new roof, call me.

DENNIS MARKEL, OWNER

fd

Enclosures

MEMORANDUM

Connor Publishing Group, Inc.

INTERNAL MEMORANDUM

TO: All Staff

FROM: Georgia Zinn *gz*

DATE: August 19, 20--

SUBJECT: Magazine Circulation

Connor Publishing Group has reached a milestone. Anita Munoz in the Circulation Department reports that our magazine circulation has reached 200,000 copies per month. This circulation level is a terrific accomplishment for a niche magazine that is just two years old.

The success of this magazine rests on all of you. Your dedication and hard work are what make this a quality magazine. Congratulations to all of you, and keep up the good work.

UNBOUND REPORT

TIPS FOR GETTING ORGANIZED

Do you have trouble getting everything done in the time available? Do you often lose important papers? Do you lose papers on top of your desk? If you are like most people, the answer to some of these questions is a resounding yes! Perhaps a few tips for getting organized would be helpful.

<u>Time Inventory</u>

Record on a time log the amount of time you spend each day in various activities. Do this for a week. Then analyze your time log to discover ways in which you can improve the management of your time. Ask yourself these questions:

1. What is generally my most productive period of the day? Why?

2. What is my least productive period of the day? Why?

3. When do I waste time? On what tasks or activities do I waste time?

4. On what activities could I spend less time and still get the desired results?

5. Do I have all my supplies and materials ready before beginning an activity?

After you have analyzed your time log, focus first on your time wasters.

<u>Identify your time wasters.</u> Some time wasters may be external factors that you cannot easily control, such as telephone interruptions, meetings, and socializing. However, you can control internal factors, such as procrastination and failure to delegate, plan, or set priorities.

Once you identify your time wasters, figure out how to minimize them. You might screen calls to cut down on telephone interruptions. Or you might schedule meetings during your less productive periods of the day, leaving your productive periods for your own use.

2

Develop a "Things to Do" List

Develop a list of tasks to be completed, placing the most urgent items first. Check your list every day, and revise as needed. Make sure, however, that you are not just shuffling the same items. Strive to cross things off the list. Then add new items to the list, always prioritizing for efficiency.

Maintain a Recording and Filing System

Keep pertinent information in an accessible place. Two such places are an electronic organizer and your personal files.

Electronic organizer. Carry a pocket organizer to keep track of appointments, expenses, addresses, telephone numbers, and reminders.

Filing system. Store important papers in one place—your files. Label folders appropriately; for example, health insurance, benefits, current project, past projects, and so on.

Time is a valuable resource of which few people have enough. The aim of time management is to provide for efficient use of resources, including time, so that individuals are more productive and less stressed.

REFERENCES

Fulton-Calkins, Patsy J., and Joanna D. Hanks. Procedures for the Office Professional, 4e. Cincinnati: South-Western Educational Publishing, 2000.

Odgers, Pattie, and B. Lewis Keeling. Administrative Office Management, 12e. Cincinnati: South-Western Educational Publishing, 2000.

"Time Management Tips." Self-Development Center. 5 Aug. 2000. George Mason University. 18 Oct. 20--. <http://www.gmu.edu/gmu/personal/time.html>.

PARTS OF A SENTENCE

7-1 Sentences contain subjects and predicates.

Subjects are the people, places, or things sentences are about.

Nouns and **pronouns** serve as the subjects of sentences. They tell what sentences are about.

Nouns are people, places, things, or concepts.

Samantha, Chicago, pizza, love

Pronouns are words used in place of nouns.

I, you, he, she, it, we, they

7-2 **Predicates** indicate what the subjects are or do. Predicates contain either action verbs or linking verbs.

Action verbs express action.

The students listened.

Action verbs often express action toward objects.

Objects answer the question *what* or *whom.*

Jamal kicked the ball.

Linking verbs connect complements to subjects.

Complements are nouns, pronouns, or adjectives that describe or rename the subject.

The flowers smell good.

The winner is he.

SUBJECT-VERB AGREEMENT

7-3 Subjects and verbs must agree in number. A singular subject must have a singular verb.

Omar tell funny jokes.

A plural subject must have a plural verb.

Omar's jokes makes me laugh.

The pronouns *he, she, it,* and *I* are singular. The pronoun *you* may be singular or plural, but it always requires a plural verb. *I* requires a plural verb. The pronouns *we* and *they* are plural.

Connie work at the diner at night.

It take about an hour to get there.

You hopes to get a job.

I mows lawns on weekends.

They wonders when the parade starts.

7-4 In a **compound subject** two or more subjects perform the action of the verb. Elements of a compound subject joined by *and* require a plural verb.

Mom and Dad has a meeting tonight.

The writer and the proofreader is working hard.

Answers: 7-3: tells, make, works, takes, hope, mow, wonder; 7-4: have, are

SUBJECT-VERB AGREEMENT
(continued)

7-5   If the elements of a compound subject are joined by *or* or *nor,* the verb must agree with the subject that is nearest the verb.

> Scott or Dee usually practice after school.

> Dad or the Zellers takes me to camp.

> Neither she nor I likes riding the bus.

7-6   Ignore words or word groups that come between subjects and verbs to find true subjects and verbs.

> Our teachers, together with our principal, encourages us to achieve high standards.

7-7   Look for the true subject after the verb in sentences that are in inverted order.

> There is cars and trucks to be parked.

> Did Tess gives you her e-mail address?

7-8   Decide whether the members of a **collective noun,** which identifies a group, act as one unit (singular verb) or as individuals (plural verb).

> An audience rise for a standing ovation.

> I think the committee meet after lunch.

Answers: 7-5: practices, take, like; 7-6: encourage; 7-7: are, give; 7-8: rises, meets

SUBJECT-VERB AGREEMENT
(continued)

7-9   Use a singular verb with the subject *the number.* Use a plural verb with the subject *a number.*

> The number of hatchlings increase daily.

> A number of hatchlings is growing their feathers.

7-10   The noun following a fraction expression indicates whether to use a singular or plural verb. If the noun is singular, use a singular verb; if plural, use a plural verb.

> One-third of the class are on a field trip.

> Two-thirds of the students is absent today.

7-11   If a quantity or measurement is a total amount, use a singular verb.

> Twenty-four square feet are the minimum space for a booth at the Fun Fair.

If a quantity or measurement is a number of counted items, use a plural verb.

> Two tables is needed for each booth.

Answers: 7-9: increases, are; 7-10: is, are; 7-11: is, are

SUBJECT-VERB AGREEMENT
(continued)

7-12 **Indefinite pronouns,** which are not specific pronouns but refer to other nouns, may be the subjects of sentences. Most of the common indefinite pronouns require singular verbs.

> Everyone are ready to go.

> Neither of our addresses are published yet.

> Let me know if anyone calls on the phone.

The indefinite pronouns *both, few, many, others,* and *several* are always plural.

> Few of us has all the right answers.

> Others is always asking me for my opinion.

> We heard several sing during the last hour.

The indefinite pronouns *all, any, more, most, none,* and *some* may be singular or plural. If the noun following the pronoun is singular, use a singular verb; if plural, use a plural verb.

> Most of the food are left over.

> Most of the employees agrees on the policy.

> Some of the recipes is available online.

> Some of the money are earmarked for the women's shelter.

Answers: 7-12: Everyone is, Neither is, C, Few have, Others are, C, Most of the food is, Most of the employees agree, Some of the recipes are, Some of the money is

SENTENCE FAULTS

7-13 A **sentence fragment** lacks either a subject or a verb and does not express a complete thought.

> Laid the books on the table.

> Kiko and Jenna on the top floor.

> Daniel speaking.

A **comma splice** contains two complete thoughts incorrectly joined by a comma.

> The deadline is 5 p.m., after that the project will be late.

> Mr. Bradshaw set the deadline, we need to meet it.

A **run-on sentence** contains two complete thoughts incorrectly joined without punctuation.

> The deadline is 5 p.m. after that the project will be late.

> Mr. Bradshaw set the deadline we need to meet it.

Answers: 7-13: *missing a subject, missing a verb, does not express a complete thought, . . . 5 p.m. After that . . . , . . . deadline. We need . . . , . . . 5 p.m. After that . . . , . . . deadline. We need . . .*

PRONOUNS

Personal Pronouns			
Case	**Person**	**Singular**	**Plural**
Nominative (Subjective)	1	I	we
	2	you	you
	3	he, she, it	they
Objective	1	me	us
	2	you	you
	3	him, her, it	them
Possessive	1	my, mine	our(s)
	2	your(s)	your(s)
	3	his, her(s), its	their(s)
Reflexive	1	myself	ourselves
	2	yourself	yourselves
	3	himself, herself, itself	themselves

Indefinite Pronouns				Always Plural	Singular or Plural Depending on Antecedent
Always Singular				**Always Plural**	**Singular or Plural Depending on Antecedent**
another	everybody	none		both	all
anybody	everyone	no one		few	any
anyone	everything	nothing		many	more
anything	many a/an	one		others	most
each	much	somebody		several	none
either	neither	someone			some
every	nobody	something			

PRONOUN EXERCISES

8-1   A pronoun must agree with its antecedent in number and gender.

> The boys were hungry when he came for dinner.

If the antecedent is a collective noun, decide whether the group is acting as a unit (singular) or as individuals (plural).

> The society has their meeting on Monday.

If the antecedent is an indefinite pronoun, determine whether the indefinite pronoun is singular or plural.

> Everyone has their own job to do.

> Some of the report are published online.

8-2   Use pronouns in the nominative case when the pronoun is the subject of a verb.

> Margaret said Phillipe and him left the meeting.

> Tad and her are working late tonight.

If a pronoun acts as a subject complement after a linking verb, use the nominative case.

> It was him who came up with the idea.

> Miss Meade said it was her who paid the bill.

Answers: 8-1: they, its, his or her, is; 8-2: he, she, he, she

PRONOUN EXERCISES
(continued)

8-3   Use the objective case when the pronoun is the object of a verb.

> Willa told she about the promotion.

> Taylor called Virgil and I into the meeting.

Use an objective pronoun as the object of a preposition.

> The clown delivered a balloon for her and I.

> Between you and I, that color is awful.

Use the objective case when the pronoun is the subject or the object of an infinitive.

> We hired Maria and he to cater the party.

> My dream is to fly they to the Bahamas.

8-4   Use possessive case pronouns to show ownership. Possessive pronouns do not have apostrophes.

> It was their proposal.

> Each locker had it's own decoration.

Use a possessive pronoun before a gerund.

> We appreciate you coming to our defense.

> Him earning a high grade increased his self-confidence.

Answers: 8-3: her, me, me, me, him, them; 8-4: C, its, your, His

PRONOUN EXERCISES

(continued)

8-5   For pronouns that precede appositives, ignore the appositive to determine the correct pronoun.

> The principal asked we freshmen to help.

> Us mail carriers are not looking forward to the holidays.

8-6   A reflexive pronoun occurs in the same sentence as the noun or pronoun to which it refers.

> I will write me a note so I don't forget.

> Send your surveys to myself for a final tally.

8-7   *Who* and *whoever* are nominative case pronouns. Use them as subjects of verbs.

> Whomever knocked at the door is gone now.

> We will contact whoever you think is best.

Whom and *whomever* are objective case pronouns. Use them as objects of verbs and prepositions.

> Hachiro is the one whom we named most efficient.

> I know whoever you choose will be the best person for the job.

Answers: 8-5: us, We; 8-6: myself, me; 8-7: Whoever, C, C, whomever

GENDER-NEUTRAL LANGUAGE EXERCISES

8-8 Avoid the use of generic masculine pronouns when gender is unknown or irrelevant.

A doctor must listen carefully to his patients.

To avoid gender-specific singular pronouns, use plural antecedents and plural pronouns.

A good nurse seldom admits she is tired.

A collie makes a good companion for his owner.

Or avoid gender-specific pronouns by eliminating the pronoun with an article.

Every team member signed his agreement.

In general, use neutral terms when choosing pronouns to identify people whose gender is unknown. Suggest alternatives to these gender-specific terms:

the best man for the job

foreman

chairman

woman's intuition

man-hours

Answers: 8-8: his or her (or Doctors . . . their), he or she (or nurses . . . they are), his or her (or Collies make good companions for their owners.), signed the (or an) agreement, the best person for the job, supervisor, chair (or chairperson), intuition, work-hours

EXERCISES FOR ERRORS IN WORDS OFTEN CONFUSED

9-1   This model represents (a/an) exceptional value.

     Is this the sort (a/of) product you had in mind?

9-2   Thank you, but I cannot (accept/except) your invitation.

9-3   Mr. Butler gave me some excellent (advice/advise).

9-4   A negative attitude will have an (adverse/averse) effect on your career.

9-5   What (affect/effect) will this promotion have on my career?

9-6   I have (all ready/already) been to the personnel office.

     Our department serves customers in (always/all ways).

9-7   I am (anxious/eager) to help you with your new job.

Answers: 9-1: an, of; 9-2: accept; 9-3: advice; 9-4: adverse; 9-5: effect;
9-6: already, all ways; 9-7: eager

EXERCISES FOR ERRORS IN WORDS OFTEN CONFUSED

(continued)

9-8   The delicious food at Shady Rest B&B helps to (assure/ensure/insure) guest satisfaction.

Marla wrote to her clients to (assure/ensure/insure) them that their money was safe.

9-9   Keillor felt (bad/badly) about his behavior.

9-10   Miss Greenbaugh had to choose (between/among) the top three candidates.

9-11   Please (bring/take) this book back to the library.

Can you (bring/take) bagels to our 6 a.m. meeting?

9-12   (Can/May) I borrow your copy of the annual report?

9-13   Tia will (cite/sight/site) her mother, who is a doctor, as a source in her biology report.

9-14   The new director of marketing, Annette Cortez, is a perfect (complement/compliment) to our department.

Answers: 9-8: ensure, assure; 9-9: bad; 9-10: among; 9-11: take, bring; 9-12: May; 9-13: cite; 9-14: complement

EXERCISES FOR ERRORS IN WORDS OFTEN CONFUSED

(continued)

9-15 As your doctor, I (council/counsel) you to exercise moderately every day.

9-16 I was responsible for balancing the firm's books (every day/everyday).

9-17 Our division has (fewer/less) management-level employees than yours.

9-18 Fernando did (good/well) on his entrance exam.

9-19 Stefan had not meant to (imply/infer) that Melanie was untrustworthy.

9-20 Duane said he did (lay/lie) the package on the workroom table.

9-21 If we do not (loose/lose) the Varbonovich account, we might be eligible for a bonus.

9-22 As in (passed/past) years, we will delay the company holiday party until January.

Answers: 9-15: counsel; 9-16: every day; 9-17: fewer; 9-18: well; 9-19: imply; 9-20: lay; 9-21: lose; 9-22: past

EXERCISES FOR ERRORS IN WORDS OFTEN CONFUSED

(continued)

9-23 Her speech will (precede/proceed) Mr. Sugihara's presentation.

9-24 The safety of our workers is our (principal/principle) concern.

9-25 The cold front was (stationary/stationery) today, but tomorrow it will begin to move through the area.

9-26 The report (that/which/who) was due March 15 is behind schedule.

    The Nelson Dam project report, (that/which/who) was due March 15, is behind schedule.

    The speaker (that/which/who) canceled was noted to be very motivational.

9-27 I was (to/too/two) tired to argue the point further.

Answers: 9-23: precede; 9-24: principal; 9-25: stationary; 9-26: that, which, who; 9-27: too

WORDS DESERVING SPECIAL CONSIDERATION

9-28 Choose words from the following list to insert in the blanks below:

alright/all right   like/as   retroactive to/for

etc./and so on   irregardless/   unique
                      regardless

Now that the new schedule is in place, the work hours seem to be ___________________ with everyone. Complaints regarding work hours are hardly ___________________ to our company. ___________________ of how much satisfaction they get from their jobs, ___________________ most workers, our employees would rather spend time at home enjoying their families, friends, hobbies, ___________________. The policy regarding compensation for the new work hours is ___________________ the first of the month.

Answers: all right, unique, Regardless, like, and so on, retroactive to

TERMINAL PUNCTUATION EXERCISES

10-1 Statements, commands, indirect questions, and polite requests end with a period.

A cold front will pass through this afternoon

Welcome to our third annual meeting

Mrs. Bartelt asked if anyone had other ideas

Would you please clean out the garage

10-2 Direct questions end with a question mark.

Do you have your monthly figures completed

Did you wonder why we went over budget

It seems as if the project is flowing smoothly, don't you agree

10-3 Sentences or introductory words that express strong emotion, surprise, or urgency end with an exclamation point.

Do not enter this chamber without proper safety equipment

Oh That's a terrific idea

Answers: 10-1: afternoon.; meeting.; ideas.; garage.; 10-2: completed?; budget?; agree?; 10-3: equipment!; Oh!; idea. (or idea!)

INTERNAL PUNCTUATION EXERCISES

10-4 A comma separates a name or title in direct address.

> Let me know if you can attend Sandy.

> However Mr. Chan the idea is still valid.

10-5 A comma sets off contrasted elements.

> The keynote speaker's session though poorly attended was well received.

10-6 A comma provides clarity and prevents misreading.

> Outside the toddler crawled in the grass under her mother's watchful eye.

> For Eric Marshall worked hard and proved himself worthy of the job.

10-7 A comma separates identical words, except when the comma might cause confusion.

> The click click of the wall clock was annoying.

> What it was was a completely new method of project management.

Answers: 10-4: attend, Sandy; However, Mr. Chan, the; 10-5: session, though poorly attended, was; 10-6: Outside, the; Eric, Marshall; 10-7: click, click; was, was

INTERNAL PUNCTUATION EXERCISES
(continued)

10-8   A comma indicates omitted words.

Last quarter's sales were $2.7 million; this quarter's $2.4 million.

10-9   A comma separates two adjectives that modify the same noun.

This has been an exciting profitable year.

Anna is a solid hard-working employee.

10-10   A comma separates adjacent unrelated numbers when both are either words or figures.

As of December 31 234 employees will be transferred to San Francisco.

Before five six dock workers need to clock out.

10-11   A comma separates two or more parts of an address. A comma separates city and state names.

Please forward my mail to 442 Greenleaf Avenue Wilmette Illinois 60091-1910.

In Pittsburgh Pennsylvania three great rivers meet.

Answers: 10-8: this quarter's, $2.4; 10-9: exciting, profitable; solid, hard-working; 10-10: December 31, 234; five, six; 10-11: Avenue, Wilmette, Illinois; Pittsburgh, Pennsylvania, three

INTERNAL PUNCTUATION EXERCISES
(continued)

10-12   Commas separate three or more elements of a date.

The launch meeting is Tuesday July 17.

On Wednesday July 18 we will sign the contract.

10-13   A comma separates names from professional designations and personal titles.

Ian Malloy Esq. is the newly appointed counsel.

Louisa Baez D.D.S. announces the opening of her new practice.

10-14   A comma separates introductory words from a quotation.

Samir whispered "Is this movie ever going to end?"

10-15   A comma separates items in a series.

Bill Tammy and Mia all went to the briefing.

I can mail the report to you transmit it by fax or deliver it in person.

Answers: 10-12: Tuesday, July 17; Wednesday, July 18, we; 10-13: Malloy, Esq., is; Baez, D.D.S., announces; 10-14: whispered, "Is; 10-15: Bill, Tammy, and Mia; you, transmit it by fax, or

INTERNAL PUNCTUATION EXERCISES
(continued)

10-16   A comma separates the main clauses of a compound sentence.

> Bridget has the expertise but Nicole has the interpersonal skills for the job.

> Ken will attend the team meeting or Shawnel will fill him in later.

10-17   A comma separates introductory elements from the rest of the sentence.

> However the deadline may be extended.

> After the first of the year we will be in a better position to hire new employees.

> Having completed his assignment early Ricardo volunteered for more work.

10-18   A comma separates an introductory or internal dependent clause from the rest of the sentence.

> While you are in Cleveland be sure to visit the Rock and Roll Hall of Fame and Museum.

> The Children's Museum of Indianapolis which is open daily is well worth your time.

Answers: 10-16: expertise, but; attend, or; 10-17: However, the; year, we; early, Ricardo; 10-18: Cleveland, be; Indianapolis, which is open daily, is

INTERNAL PUNCTUATION EXERCISES
(continued)

10-19   A comma is not used after a phrase or clause that functions as a subject.

   Whatever he knows is a mystery to the rest of us.

10-20   A comma sets off nonessential elements.

   Dr. Nguyen whose clinic is downtown just hired a new partner.

   Do not use a comma to set off essential elements.

   The clinic that is operated by Dr. Nguyen offers free services to needy children.

10-21   A comma sets off nonessential parenthetical expressions.

   This link for example takes you to our home page.

   Therefore profits are down compared to the previous fiscal year.

10-22   A comma sets off appositives.

   Carly Heilman a new associate will take her first case to court today.

Answers: 10-19: C; 10-20: Nguyen, whose clinic is downtown, just; C; 10-21: link, for example, takes; Therefore, profits; 10-22: Heilman, a new associate, will

EXERCISES FOR SEMICOLONS

11-1   A semicolon separates independent clauses in a compound sentence without a conjunction.

> We need to hold an orientation session we have four new hires in our department.

> Let me know when you schedule the session I'll send a memo to the new employees.

11-2   A semicolon separates independent clauses in a compound sentence that are joined by a conjunction when one of the clauses contains internal commas.

> Human Resources asked Marian, Delaney, and Raul to attend but none of them can do so.

11-3   A semicolon separates clauses in a compound sentence when the clauses are joined by an adverbial conjunction or a transitional phrase.

> No one could attend therefore the session was rescheduled.

> Selma organized the meeting room in the meantime Julius ushered in the guests.

11-4   A semicolon separates items in a list when one or more of those items contain an internal comma.

> The cities we are considering are Chicago, Illinois; Helena, Montana; and Hartford, Connecticut.

Answers: 11-1: session; we / session; I'll / 11-2: attend; but / 11-3: attend; therefore, the / room; in the meantime, Julius / 11-4: C

EXERCISES FOR COLONS

11-5 A colon introduces a question or a quotation of two or more sentences.

> Mr. Arbelias asked: "How do we ensure the quality of our product? This is our new priority."

11-6 A colon follows a clause that introduces another explanatory or defining clause.

> His approach was simple: Keep the customers happy by telling them whatever they want to hear.

11-7 A colon introduces a horizontal or vertical list or series.

> The planning stage requires many considerations namely, schedule, staff, and budget.

11-8 A colon separates hours and minutes in numerical time expressions.

> My lecture starts at 8:30 a.m. and ends at 1 p.m.

11-9 In business letters colons are used with reference initials (if the author's initials appear) and are used following a salutation (using mixed punctuation).

> Dear Senator Carlisle: dlr:sm

Answers: 11-5: C; 11-6: C; 11-7: considerations: namely, schedule; 11-8: C; 11-9: C

EXERCISES FOR APOSTROPHES

11-10   Use an apostrophe and *s* to form the possessive

11-11   case of a singular noun that does not end in an *s*

11-12   sound, an indefinite pronoun, or an irregular noun (singular or plural).

> One students attention wandered during lecture.
>
> Someones dog is in the childrens playhouse.

11-13   To form the possessive of compound nouns, make the final element possessive.

> The editor-in-chiefs decision is final.

11-14   To show joint ownership, make the final name possessive. To show separate ownership, make each name possessive.

> Drew and Tally's new truck is bright red.
>
> Coreys and Terells jobs are interesting.

11-15   Use an apostrophe to form the plural of all lowercase letters and the capital letters A, I, M, and U.

> Your gs look like qs.

11-16   Use an apostrophe to indicate omitted letters or figures.

> couldnt   class of 08   o'clock

Answers: 11-10–11-12: student's, Someone's, children's; 11-13: editor-in-chief's; 11-14: C, Corey's and Terell's; 11-15: g's, q's; 11-16: couldn't, '08, C

EXERCISES FOR QUOTATION MARKS

11-17   Quotation marks identify a direct quotation.

> According to Deb, All employees receive a raise of at least 4 percent on their fifth service anniversary.

11-18   Single quotation marks enclose a quotation within a quotation.

> My grandmother once said to me, "Your motto should be the words of Eleanor Roosevelt, The future belongs to those who believe in the beauty of their dreams.

11-19   Quotation marks identify titles of book chapters, article titles, and other parts of complete works.

> Read Chapter 2, "Speaking in Public," by next Wednesday.

> By Thursday read the article titled Impress Your Audience that I handed out yesterday.

11-20   Quotation marks identify words or phrases used in special ways.

> Some corporate training is called suitcasing because it requires the instructor to travel.

Answers: 11-17: Deb, "All . . . anniversary."; 11-18: 'The . . . dreams.'"
11-19: C, "Impress Your Audience"; 11-20: "suitcasing"

EXERCISES FOR UNDERSCORES AND ITALICS

11-21 Underscore or italicize the titles of books, journals, magazines, newspapers, and audio and video recordings.

> This month's Business Today has an article about working from home.

> The reviewer for The Times gave Clinton's book, It Takes a Village, a good review.

Underscore or italicize the titles of plays, movies, and musical compositions.

> While in New York City, I saw live performances of 42nd Street and Annie.

11-22 Underscore or italicize words being emphasized, defined, referred to, or used as examples.

> I said the class was in Room 232, not Room 323.

> The word volunteer comes from a Latin word that means "to will" or "to wish."

> The young contestant put an extra *c* in the word *recommend.*

Answers: 11-21: *Business Today, The Times, It Takes a Village, 42nd Street, Annie;* 11-22: Room *232,* not Room *323, volunteer,* C

EXERCISES FOR THE DASH

11-23   A dash shows a sudden change in thought.

My thought and this is putting it politely was that this job was definitely not for me.

11-24   A dash can emphasize a nonessential element.

No one can blame you well, that's not true.

11-25   A dash can provide a strong, informal break between two independent clauses.

We shouldn't stereotype students at the university though most engineering students fit the mold.

11-26   A dash can be a strong, informal introduction to
11-27   explanatory material. A dash separates a list from explanatory text that follows it.

The obstacles between my degree and me were significant financing, holding down a job, and road construction on I-77.

Books, lab fees, supplies a student's expenses are many.

11-28   Use a dash before an author's name when attributing a quotation.

Youth is like spring; an overpraised season.
—Samuel Butler

Answers: 11-23: thought—and this is putting it politely—was; 11-24: you—well, that's; 11-25: university—though; 11-26–11-27: significant—financing, supplies—a student's; 11-28: C

EXERCISES FOR PARENTHESES

11-29 Use parentheses to set off nonessential extra information.

> To locate our booth, enter the exhibit hall from the east entrance by the parking lot and turn right.

> While you are reading the report, you can refer to the maps in the appendix for reference. (The appendix appears at the end of the report.)

11-30 Enclose an explanation for an abbreviation or a period of time in parentheses.

> CAS Chemical Abstracts Service catalogs and stores scientific information from all over the world.

> During her reign 1558–1603, Queen Elizabeth maintained a vast empire.

11-31 Use parentheses to enclose characters in a run-in enumeration.

> To prepare for my class, you should 1 read my book, 2 read it again, and 3 memorize all underlined text.

Answers: 11-29: (by the parking lot), C; 11-30: CAS (Chemical Abstracts Service), reign (1558–1603), Queen Elizabeth; 11-31: should (1) read my book, (2) read it again, and (3) memorize

EXERCISES FOR BRACKETS

11-32 Enclose in brackets information presented within a quotation that was not part of the original quote.

> Mrs. Callahan reported, "At the end of this fiscal year [2006], Callahan Inc. will merge with Carveen Landscaping."

11-33 Enclose the word *sic* in brackets to indicate an error in an original source.

> During her interview Janell stated, "I am a proud alumni [*sic*] of Washington University."

11-34 Enclose in brackets information about changes made to a quotation for emphasis.

> In his article Tirso states, "The governor issued a stay of sentence <u>three days</u> before hearing the court's final verdict." Emphasis added.

Answers: 11-32: C; 11-33: C; 11-34: . . . final verdict." [Emphasis added.]

CAPITALIZATION EXERCISES

12-1   Capitalize the first word of a sentence, a question, a direct quotation, and a phrase or single word that expresses a complete thought.

> everyone in our group enjoyed the festivities.

> can you believe this?

> Over the loudspeaker the principal said, "this year's award-winning student volunteer is Leon Nolan."

> fantastic!

Do not capitalize the first word of the second part of an interrupted quotation.

> "Corporate mergers," stated the new chief executive, "Are inevitable."

12-2   Capitalize the first word after a colon if that word begins a complete sentence.

> Today was Nieca's last day of work: she retired.

> Please order four items from our supplier: Copier toner, yellow printer paper, shipping labels, and hanging file folders.

Answers: 12-1: Everyone, Can, "This, Fantastic!, are; 12-2: She, copier

CAPITALIZATION EXERCISES
(continued)

12-3   Capitalize people's names.

> Please join me in welcoming lisa qualley to our Editorial Department.

12-4   Capitalize personal or professional titles that appear before a person's name, either in text or in an address.

> Last year mr. Rotolo started his own business.

> The school board reports that superintendent Torres has announced her retirement.

> We invited senator Deborah Pryce to be our commencement speaker.

Do not capitalize a title when it follows a person's name or is used in place of the name.

> Parker Alexander, the Governor, will announce his plans at tomorrow's press conference.

> The Assistant Vice President has agreed to our request for flextime.

Answers: 12-3: Lisa Qualley; 12-4: Mr. Rotolo, Superintendent Torres, Senator Deborah Pryce, the governor, The assistant vice president

CAPITALIZATION EXERCISES
(continued)

12-5   Capitalize proper nouns and the personal pronoun *I*.

> The factory where i used to work is now a part of millennium marketplace.

12-6   Capitalize proper adjectives.

> His trek through the alaskan wilderness was a life-changing experience.

12-7   In hyphenated words capitalize only those parts that are proper nouns or proper adjectives.

> The restaurant serves this city's best mexican-american cuisine.

> By Mid-September the leaves begin to turn.

12-8   Capitalize the first and last words and all important words in titles. Articles, conjunctions, and short prepositions are not capitalized.

> I try to read *the wall street journal* every day.

> After reading *what color is your parachute?*, I knew I wanted to be a veterinarian.

> Please read "casual dress at work" before the company's policy goes into effect.

Answers: 12-5: I, Millennium Marketplace; 12-6: Alaskan; 12-7: Mexican-American cuisine, mid-September; 12-8: *The Wall Street Journal, What Color Is Your Parachute?,* "Casual Dress at Work"

CAPITALIZATION EXERCISES
(continued)

12-9   Capitalize names of organizations.

> The american museum of natural history was founded in 1869.

> Capitalize names of specific departments or groups within the originator's own company, but not those of another organization.

>> I reported my lost paycheck to the accounting department.

>> I called for service on our broken copier and spoke to someone in Customer Service.

12-10   Capitalize specific brand names, but do not capitalize the product words.

>> I listen to my Walkman Stereo when I ride the bus.

12-11   Capitalize points of the compass when they refer to regions or are part of a proper noun. Do not capitalize these words when they indicate a direction.

>> Go to the northeast to study America's history.

>> Freshmen classes are usually on south campus.

>> The office park is a half mile West of the river.

Answers: 12-9: American Museum of Natural History, Accounting Department, customer service; 12-10: Walkman stereo; 12-11: Northeast, South Campus, west

CAPITALIZATION EXERCISES
(continued)

12-12 Capitalize seasons of the year *only* when they are part of a proper noun.

> After a long Winter, we look forward to the annual spring ragtime review in April.

12-13 Capitalize names of days of the week, months of the year, and holidays.

> Jude's service anniversary is next tuesday, which happens to be april fools' day.

12-14 Capitalize an academic degree when it immediately follows a person's name. Do not capitalize a degree name when it is used in general terms or with the word *degree.*

> Our newest doctor is Tim Vasathan, d.v.m., who received his Veterinary Degree last May.

12-15 Capitalize names of specific course titles. Do not capitalize general areas of study unless the name includes a proper noun or proper adjective.

> I enrolled in applied business communication 231 to improve my writing skills.

> I hope to study european history.

Answers: 12-12: winter, Spring Ragtime Review; 12-13: Tuesday, April Fools' Day; 12-14: D.V.M., veterinary degree; 12-15: Applied Business Communication 231; European history

CAPITALIZATION EXERCISES

(continued)

12-16   Capitalize most nouns followed by numbers. Do not capitalize the words *line, note, page, paragraph, size, step,* and *verse.*

> In the itinerary on Page 4, Paragraph 3, you will find these directions: Take highway 51 north for about 14 miles; then exit on state road 2.

12-17   Capitalize the first word of each item in a displayed (vertical) list.

> Following are the parts that were missing from the tricycle (Model 531D) I purchased:
>
> > handlebar grips (2)
> >
> > wheel hub (1)

12-18   In an outline, first-level headings are in all capital letters. Second-level headings have all main words in initial capital letters. Third-level and subsequent headings have only the first word capitalized.

> I.   project management
> >   A. budget planning and accounting
> >   B. scheduling
> > >   1. locating resources
> > >   2. hiring personnel
> >   C. coordinating staff and vendors

Answers: 12-16: page 4, paragraph 3, Highway 51, State Road 2; 12-17: Handlebar, Wheel; 12-18: PROJECT MANAGEMENT, Budget Planning and Accounting, Scheduling, Locating resources, Hiring personnel, Coordinating Staff and Vendors

EDITING FOR CONTENT

13-1   Proofread for inaccuracies in dates, figures, addresses, names, and numbers. If necessary, query the originator.

> Contact the humane society by calling 1-800-555-PETS. That's 1-800-555-7388.
>
> TO: Collin DiMarco
>
> FROM: Sylvie Alonzo
>
> DATE: Thursday, July 16, 20--
>
> SUBJECT: Insurance Policy
>
> In accordance with our phone conversation on Wednesday, July 14, your monthly premium will be withdrawn directly from your bank account. The first automatic transaction will take place in August. Please submit a regular payment to cover your July premium. Please let me know if I can be of further assistance, Mr. DiMarco.
>
> The company is now located at 2741 Wendell Road, Pontiac, MI 48341-126.
>
> If that paper is 10 percent off the regular price, then a carton that usually costs $23.70 will cost only $21.18.

Answers: 13-1: 1-800-555-7387; Wednesday, July 15; 48341-126 /?; $21.33

EDITING FOR CONTENT
(continued)

13-2   Proofread for inconsistencies by paying special attention to names and titles, figures, and format.

Sylvie,

Collin DiMarco wants to switch to automatic withdrawal. Please call him at his office number today to make the arrangements. Mr. DeMarco has just purchased his policy, so he may have other questions as well.

Kathryn O'Dell has resurrected the old diner building at Second and Main. The grand opening of Katherine's O'Deli has put a spark of life into the downtown lunch scene.

On the web site's home page, click on "Breed Profiles" to learn about every breed of dog. This is the only Website that includes such complete breed information.

13-3   Proofread for missing information.

The historical society is at the corner of Parker Street.

Travel expense reports are due within three following the travel for which the expense report is being submitted.

Answers: 13-2: DiMarco, DeMarco /?; Kathryn, Katherine's /?; web site, Website /?; 13-3: corner of Parker Street /and?; within three /?

EDITING FOR CONCISENESS

14-1   Edit clichés and imprecise words.

> We need to take the bull by the horns at the organizational meeting today.

> Dave knew he was going to face the music someday.

> I thought it was a good meeting.

14-2   Edit obsolete expressions.

> TO: Natalie Boerner
> FROM: Millicent O'Keefe
> DATE: Tuesday, August 7, 20--
> SUBJECT: Contacting Clients
>
> Due to the fact that the office will be closed in the near future while new carpeting is being installed, I would like to ask that you call clients who have appointments that day to reschedule. Attached herewith is a copy of my schedule for August. I would appreciate it very much if you would take the liberty to reschedule these clients in accordance with their schedules and mine. Please make these calls at your earliest convenience.

Sample Answers: 14-1: We need to take charge at the organizational meeting today. Dave knew he was going to face the consequences of his actions. I thought it was a productive meeting. 14-2: Because the office will be closed on Friday, August 17, while new carpeting is being installed, please call clients who have appointments that day to reschedule. Attached is a copy of my schedule for August. I would appreciate your rescheduling these clients according to their schedules and mine. Please make these calls by the end of this week.

EDITING FOR CONCISENESS
(continued)

14-3   Edit for wordy or redundant expressions.

The ink marks on that cover page are visible to the eye.

It is my personal opinion that all parking spots should be charged at the same dollar amount.

You should make a note that these procedures are exactly identical except for the numbering.

I am writing this memo to inform you that the administrative office meeting originally scheduled to be held this Wednesday has been changed to next Wednesday. Please make plans to attend.

14-4   Edit for passive voice.

The combination to the safe is known only to three people.

Arturo was hired to replace Freeman last November.

The editors were taught how to create an automatic table of contents. Instruction on how to create one can be obtained from any of them.

Sample Answers: 14-3: The ink marks on that cover page are visible. It is my opinion [or I think] that all parking spots should be charged at the same amount. Please note that these procedures are identical except for the numbering. The administrative office meeting scheduled for this Wednesday has been changed to next Wednesday. Please plan to attend. 14-4: Only three people know the combination to the safe. [Our director] hired Arturo to replace Freeman last November. [Margo] taught the editors how to create an automatic table of contents. Any of the editors can instruct you on how to create one.

EDITING FOR CLARITY

15-1   Edit misplaced and dangling modifiers.

I only have one dollar in my purse.

(I mean to say that one dollar is the only money I have in my purse.)

If you ask for my help, I will be happy to assist you in the morning.

(I mean to say that I will help you the morning you ask for help, not the morning after you ask.)

15-2   Edit dangling modifiers that follow introductory phrases. (For this exercise keep the introductory phrases and edit the remainder.)

Singing loudly, Lassie was taken by his owner on a leisurely stroll through the park.

Locked in the car, Terron knew that set of keys was her only one.

To earn a promotion, every effort must be made to meet the criteria.

Filling in for the accounts manager, the customer was not happy with Vince's decision.

Sample Answers: 15-1: I have only one dollar in my purse. If you ask for my help in the morning, I will be happy to assist you. 15-2: Singing loudly, Lassie's owner took Lassie on a leisurely stroll through the park. Locked in the car, that set of keys was the only one Terron had. To earn a promotion, you must make every effort to meet the criteria. Filling in for the accounts manager, Vince made a decision that displeased the customer.

EDITING FOR CLARITY
(continued)

15-3   Edit for parallel construction.

Marilyn furnished her new apartment by shopping garage sales, going to estate sales, and she attended auctions.

15-4   Edit for conjunctions used in pairs.

The CEO not only visited us when we introduced our new product line but also during Mr. Goto's retirement party.

15-5   Edit for simple words.

We are cognizant that we need to expedite our deliveries.

15-6   Edit for strong verbs.

To bring about a change in the sick leave policy would take the board making a determination on the effectiveness of the existing policy.

Sample Answers: 15-3: Marilyn furnished her new apartment by shopping garage sales, going to estate sales, and attending auctions. 15-4: The CEO visited us not only when we introduced our new product line but also when we hosted Mr. Goto's retirement party. 15-5: We know that we need to speed up our deliveries. 15-6: To change the sick leave policy would require the board to determine the effectiveness of the existing policy.

CHAPTER QUIZZES/
TESTS AND SOLUTIONS

Name _______________________________

*Proofread each of the following sentences for mechanical errors (spelling, abbreviation, word division, number expression, grammar, punctuation, capitalization), content errors, conciseness, and clarity. Write in your corrections. Sentences often contain more than one correction. Indicate a correct sentence by writing **C** after it. Each sentence is worth two points.*

1. While waiting for the plane, my baggage was stolen.
2. Everyone except Gil Johnson and he joined the organization.
3. The governor of Georgia traveled to Europe to seek industry for the state.
4. 15 class members participated in the rally; thats more than half the class.
5. The clerk was insistant that those 3 sweaters I bought during the Fall sale could not be returned for any reason.
6. I would like to hire Celeste Dunlap, who all ready has had three year's experience.
7. If you move to Washington, please give me a call.
8. The board voted it's approval of the preformance of the company's officers.
9. Neither Enjou nor Tai are enrolled in Accounting 411, a graduation requirement.
10. I plan to take a cruise before the cruise company's special expires; however, circumstances prevent my going at this time.
11. Bette assured me that the idea to go rafting was her's.
12. The administrative assistant, as well as the office manager, is attending the time management seminar.
13. The State of Florida is also known as the Sunshine State.
14. Peter and Doris's car cost $20,000, and they obtained a loan with 7.5% interest.
15. In Chapter 4, page 41, the following rule appears—Do not divide a word containing 6 or fewer letters.
16. A number of responses has been recieved from the Febuary 5th mailing.
17. The employment survey which traced thirty-three types of information in editorial ads, revealed several key findings.
18. On June 1, 20-- I will travel to Hawaii for a three-week vacation.
19. You should select a paralegal program created, taught and graded by experienced attorneys.
20. Chi, Julie, and Brett has gone to the hardware store to buy five gals. of paint.
21. Installing a computer in our records management department, will increase its efficiency.
22. I clearly marked the box "Fragile," but the contents were broken when I looked inside.
23. Of all the communication books you sent me, there was only one I *liked—Improving Business Writing*.
24. Here is the brochure and the check that was omitted from your letter.
25. Ham and eggs is a traditional breakfast dish in the South.
26. Isn't this where your college roommate, Stu Muldar, lives?
27. Rosangela, I found three quarters, one dime, and twelve pennies—a total of 92 cents.

28. A County prosecutor appeared in a case before the California supreme court.

29. The news bullentin reported that Gen. Hochstettler's plane would arrive at Kennedy International Airport at 10:15 a.m.

30. There will, undoubtly, be a charge for maintenance after the warranty expires.

31. She is a legal secretary in a Chicago law firm, and wants to join a professional association.

32. If you enjoy running check with your local runner's association about referral services in other cities.

33. Daylon exclaimed, "Stop. The drawbridge is open!

34. The spelling test included these words: similar, accomodate, decision, and proceedure.

35. The old, dilapidated house will be replaced by a lovely two-story house.

36. The word *telecommuting* has now become a part of the office worker's everyday vocabulary and should be a familar term to all involved in the business world.

37. Before the consultant arrives find out why shes coming.

38. Interior folders come in the same colors as hanging folders, but there just a bit shorter.

39. Today's manager has to juggle dozen's of tasks.

40. A Mid-August survey revealed that many Americans declared French fries to be they're favorite food.

41. The travel agent said, "Your final payment for the November 1 cruise is due on October 1, which is sixty days before departure."

42. In Math 465, 49 percent of the class fialed the final exam.

43. Answering the telephone and filing is considered a routine office task.

44. Ms. Dorinda Ramseyer, a Yale alumnus, received her m.a. from Duke university and was recommmended for a doctoral fellowship by Dr. D. R. Branyon.

45. If your voice tends to drop as you utter the expression, then the expression is nonessential, if your voice tends to rise, the expression is essential.

46. Evan's job was to supervise a force of 6 salespeople in the southwest.

47. Scanning her schedule once more, Abilene decided to eat lunch at her desk.

48. We work for a small ten employees, relatively new advertising agency.

49. My guess is that all of you—president and creative professionals alike are younger than your counterparts at Kato and Associates.

50. The immediate task for mangers is to get family issues on the company agenda.

Name ___________________

*Proofread each of the following sentences for mechanical errors (spelling, abbreviation, word division, number expression, grammar, punctuation, capitalization), content errors, conciseness, and clarity. Write in your corrections. Sentences often contain more than one correction. Indicate a correct sentence by writing **C** after it. Each sentence is worth two points.*

1. While waiting for the plane, my baggage was stolen. [*I was* inserted]

2. Everyone except Gil Johnson and ~~he~~ [*him*] joined the organization.

3. The governor of Georgia traveled to Europe to seek industry for the state.

4. (15) class members participated in the rally; thats more than half the class.

5. The clerk was insistant [*e*] that those 3 sweaters I bought during the Fall sale could not be returned for any reason.

6. I would like to hire Celeste Dunlap, who all ready has had three years experience.

7. If you move to Washington, please give me a call. **C**

8. The board voted its approval of the performance of the company's officers.

9. Neither Enjou nor Tai ~~are~~ [*is*] enrolled in Accounting 411, a graduation requirement.

10. I plan to take a cruise before the cruise company's special expires; however, circumstances prevent my going at this time. **C**

11. Bette assured me that the idea to go rafting was her's.

12. The administrative assistant, as well as the office manager, is attending the time management seminar. **C**

13. The State of Florida is also known as the Sunshine State.

14. Peter and Doris's car cost $20,000, and they obtained a loan with 7.5% interest.

15. In Chapter 4, page 41, the following rule appears—Do not divide a word containing 6 or fewer letters.

16. A number of responses ~~has~~ [*have*] been recieved from the Febuary 5th mailing.

17. The employment survey which traced ~~thirty-three~~ [*33*] types of information in editorial ads, revealed several key findings.

18. On June 1, 20--, I will travel to Hawaii for a three-week vacation.

19. You should select a paralegal program created, taught and graded by experienced attorneys.

20. Chi, Julie, and Brett ~~has~~ [*have*] gone to the hardware store to buy five (gals) [*or 5*] of paint.

21. Installing a computer in our records management department will increase its efficiency.

22. I clearly marked the box "Fragile," but the contents were broken when I looked inside. **C**

23. Of all the communication books you sent me, there was only one I ~~liked~~ —*Improving Business Writing.* [*No ital*]

24. Here ~~is~~ [*are*] the brochure and the check that ~~was~~ [*were*] omitted from your letter.

25. Ham and eggs is a traditional breakfast dish in the South. **C**

26. Isn't this where your college roommate, Stu Muldar, lives? **C**

27. Rosangela, I found ~~three~~ [*3*] quarters, ~~one~~ [*1*] dime, and ~~twelve~~ [*12*] pennies—a total of ~~92~~ [*97*] cents.

28. A County prosecutor appeared in a case before the California supreme court.

29. The news bulletin reported that Gen. Hochstettler's plane would arrive at Kennedy International Airport at 10:15 a.m.

30. There will, undoubtly, be a charge for maintenance after the warranty expires.

31. She is a legal secretary in a Chicago law firm, and wants to join a professional association.

32. If you enjoy running, check with your local runner's association about referral services in other cities.

33. Daylon exclaimed, "Stop! The drawbridge is open!"

34. The spelling test included these words: similar, accommodate, decision, and procedure.

35. The old, dilapidated house will be replaced by a lovely two-story house. C

36. The word *telecommuting* has now become a part of the office worker's everyday vocabulary and should be a familiar term to all involved in the business world.

37. Before the consultant arrives, find out why she's coming.

38. Interior folders come in the same colors as hanging folders, but there just a bit shorter. they're (or they are)

39. Today's manager has to juggle dozens of tasks.

40. A Mid-August survey revealed that many Americans declared French fries to be they're favorite food. their

41. The travel agent said, "Your final payment for the November 1 cruise is due on October 1, which is sixty days before departure." 30?

42. In Math 465, 49 percent of the class failed the final exam.

43. Answering the telephone and filing is considered a routine office tasks. are

44. Ms. Dorinda Ramseyer, a Yale alumnus, received her m.a. from Duke university and was recommended for a doctoral fellowship by Dr. D. R. Branyon.

45. If your voice tends to drop as you utter the expression, then the expression is nonessential; if your voice tends to rise, the expression is essential.

46. Evan's job was to supervise a force of 6 salespeople in the southwest.

47. Scanning her schedule once more, Abilene decided to eat lunch at her desk. C

48. We work for a small (ten employees), relatively new advertising agency.

49. My guess is that all of you—president and creative professionals alike, are younger than your counterparts at Kato and Associates.

50. The immediate task for mangers is to get family issues on the company agenda.

　　　　　Name ________________________________

*Use the appropriate proofreading symbols to mark all keyboarding and spelling errors. Write **C** after the sentence if it is correct.*

1. Congradulations to those of you who have made a committment to improve you proofreading skills and to make them an integral part of your work habits.

2. To be a good proofreader, on must have a keen eye and be very knowlegable about the the English language.

3. When you proofread, watch for keyboarding errors of omissions, additions, and misstrokes.

4. Proofreaders know that sometimes is it difficult to distinguish between a key boarding error and a spelling error.

5. Girard is familar with the proceedures for analysing financial reports.

6. It was almost midnight when the group reached a concensus about the contents of the knew broshure they were making for this year's holiday display.

7. I hope to persuade you to take enough cloths because the weather is so changeable.

8. Before you leave, be sure to (1) turn off the hot water, (2) close the storm windows, and and (4) leave a note for the paper carrier.

Use the appropriate proofreading symbols to mark the following sentences according to the instructions given.

9. California Coin Shop has only a few Morgan silver dollars in stock in Beverly Hills.

   Move the words *in Beverly Hills* between *Shop* and *has.* Insert the word *untouched* before the word *Morgan.*

10. I did n't see your name on the roster that Carrie uses to check names.

    Close up the space between *did* and *n't.* Cross out the name *Carrie* and insert the name *Carolyn;* then show the mark to ignore the correction and let the name *Carrie* stand.

*Use the appropriate proofreading symbols to mark all keyboarding and spelling errors. Write **C** after the sentence if it is correct.*

1. Congradulations to those of you who have made a commitment to improve your proofreading skills and to make them an integral part of your work habits.

2. To be a good proofreader, on must have a keen eye and be very knowlegable about the the English language.

3. When you proofread, watch for keyboarding errors of omissions, additions, and misstrokes. C

4. Proofreaders know that sometimes is it difficult to distinguish between a key boarding error and a spelling error.

5. Girard is familar with the proceedures for analyzing financial reports.

6. It was almost midnight when the group reached a concensus about the contents of the knew broshure they were making for this year's holiday display.

7. I hope to persuade you to take enough cloths because the weather is so changeable.

8. Before you leave, be sure to (1) turn off the hot water, (2) close the storm windows, and and (4) leave a note for the paper carrier.

Use the appropriate proofreading symbols to mark the following sentences according to the instructions given.

9. California Coin Shop has only a few Morgan silver dollars in stock in Beverly Hills.

   Move the words *in Beverly Hills* between *Shop* and *has*. Insert the word *untouched* before the word *Morgan*.

10. I did n't see your name on the roster that Carrie uses to check names.

   Close up the space between *did* and *n't*. Cross out the name *Carrie* and insert the name *Carolyn;* then show the mark to ignore the correction and let the name *Carrie* stand.

Name ___________________________

*Use the appropriate proofreading symbols to mark all abbreviation and spelling errors. Write **C** after the sentence if it is correct.*

1. The U.S. flag was flying over the embassy on Wed., August 29.

2. Washington Power&Light has a branch office in Tacoma, Washington.

3. Miguel's plane must be in St. Louis by 2 p.m. central standard time.

4. Meredith was informed by memo that she can apply for station manager at WGTC-TV.

5. The thief accidently triggered the car's security alarm.

6. You must use software that is compatible with your hardware.

7. Drs. Johansen and Melvin went deep-sea fishing aboard the *Jay IV* sometime in Sept.

8. Brian reported on the competative events for Prof. Springer's class.

9. Send a copy of the anual report to Lucas Carboni, 2613 W. Sixth Street, Dallas, TX 76201-6201.

10. Mrs. Chas. Bedford Sr., pres. of the AMA Auxiliary, is a representative to the hospital board.

11. Kay O'Reilley, Ph.D., was suprised at the number of students enrolled in the Latin class and noted that many of these students did not have the prerequisite grammer class.

12. Place the order for 5 gal. of yellow paint, 3 gal. of blue paint, 2 paint burshes, and 12 rolls of wallpaper.

Use the appropriate proofreading symbols to mark the following sentences according to the instructions given for each. Proofread for other errors as well.

13. The Gov. has agreed to be a sponser for the March of Dimes.

    Change the words *The Gov.* to read *Governor Davis.*

14. This contract is entered into by Smylie Properties as lessor and Band of Women as lessee.

    Insert the defined term *Smylie* in parentheses after the words *Smylie Properties* and the defined term *BOW* in parentheses after the words *Band of Women.*

Name _______________________

*Use the appropriate proofreading symbols to mark all abbreviation and spelling errors. Write **C** after the sentence if it is correct.*

1. The U.S. flag was flying over the embassy on Wed., August 29.

2. Washington Power & Light has a branch office in Tacoma, Washington.

3. Miguel's plane must be in St. Louis by 2 p.m. central standard time.

4. Meredith was informed by memo that she can apply for station manager at WGTC-TV. C

5. The thief accidently triggered the car's security alarm.

6. You must use software that is compatible with your hardware. C

7. Drs. Johansen and Melvin went deep-sea fishing aboard the *Jay IV* sometime in Sept.

8. Brian reported on the competitive events for Prof. Springer's class.

9. Send a copy of the anual report to Lucas Carboni, 2613 W. Sixth Street, Dallas, TX 76201-6201.

10. Mrs. Chas. Bedford Sr., pres. of the AMA Auxiliary, is a representative to the hospital board.

11. Kay O'Reilley, Ph.D., was suprised at the number of students enrolled in the Latin class and noted that many of these students did not have the prerequisite grammer class.

12. Place the order for 5 gal. of yellow paint, 3 gal. of blue paint, 2 paint brushes, and 12 rolls of wallpaper.

Use the appropriate proofreading symbols to mark the following sentences according to the instructions given for each. Proofread for other errors as well.

13. The Gov. has agreed to be a sponser for the March of Dimes.

    Change the words *The Gov.* to read *Governor Davis.*

14. This contract is entered into by Smylie Properties as lessor and Band of Women as lessee.

    Insert the defined term *Smylie* in parentheses after the words *Smylie Properties* and the defined term *BOW* in parentheses after the words *Band of Women.*

Name _______________________________

Place a check mark by the word that is correctly divided in the following word sets.

1. ___ cont- empt   ___ con- tempt
2. ___ cer- tified   ___ certi- fied
3. ___ holly- hock   ___ hol- lyhock
4. ___ sensi- tive   ___ sen- sitive
5. ___ perm- eate   ___ perme- ate
6. ___ pen- manship   ___ penman- ship
7. ___ swimm- ing   ___ swim- ming
8. ___ does- n't   ___ doesn't
9. ___ re- invest   ___ rein- vest

Place a forward slash in all the positions where the following items could be divided.

10. Governor-elect

11. http://www.georgia_peaches.com

12. Dr. Karl Watts

13. Saturday, April 10, 1985

Use the appropriate proofreading symbols to mark all word division and spelling errors. Write **C** *after the sentence if it is correct.*

14. Because our staff members are so dependible, we let them set their own schedules.

15. This is the nineth sponsored trip our company has put on the calendar; please urge Ms. Rodriquez to choose a date.

16. Last year's flood was devastating, but that experience does not compare to the $1.6 million in damages to our merchandize caused by a recent fire.

17. In the beginning days of our company, we counted all the nickles and dimes— and even pennies—but now our sales have reached a heighth we only dreamed of.

Name ______________________________

Place a check mark by the word that is correctly divided in the following word sets.

1. ___ cont- empt   ✓ con- tempt
2. ___ cer- tified   ✓ certi- fied
3. ✓ holly- hock   ___ hol- lyhock
4. ✓ sensi- tive   ___ sen- sitive
5. ___ perm- eate   ✓ perme- ate
6. ___ pen- manship   ✓ penman- ship
7. ___ swimm- ing   ✓ swim- ming
8. ___ does- n't   ✓ doesn't
9. ✓ re- invest   ___ rein- vest

Place a forward slash in all the positions where the following items could be divided.

10. Governor/elect

11. http://www/.georgia_peaches/.com

12. Dr. Karl/Watts

13. Saturday,/April 10,/1985

*Use the appropriate proofreading symbols to mark all word division and spelling errors. Write **C** after the sentence if it is correct.*

14. Because our staff members are so dependable, we let them set their own schedules.

15. This is the nineth sponsored trip our company has put on the calendar; please urge Ms. Rodriquez to choose a date.

16. Last year's flood was devastating, but that experience does not compare to the $1.6 million in damages to our merchandize caused by a recent fire.

17. In the beginning days of our company, we counted all the nickles and dimes—and even pennies—but now our sales have reached a heighth we only dreamed of.

                    Name ________________________

*Use the appropriate proofreading symbols to mark errors in the expression of numbers and in spelling. Write **C** after the sentence if it is correct.*

1. Is the Perkins' estate really worth over six million dollars?

2. More than twenty absenses will result in the loss of your license.

3. Last year 15 employees entered the marathon, but only 7 completed it.

4. One hundred seventy-eight positions were posted by Mrs. Galakatos last month.

5. Chase's new store has 16,000 square feet, a 20% increase in floor space.

6. Although Jay's nineth birthday was May 26, his party was held on June 2d.

7. Conference registration is 2 1/2 times what it was 5 years ago.

8. The swimming pool on the fourth floor of the 18-story hotel is 20 feet by 40 feet.

9. Model No. S-37,289 is described on pages 102 - 104 of the catalog.

10. Carla has accummulated almost thirty thousand frequent flyer points.

11. The principal is conscious of the need for fifty 100-page theme books.

12. More than 1/2 of homeowners have morgages on their residences.

13. Please contribute $5.00 toward the party to celebrate the team's 30th win.

14. By 8 o'clock three buses, 14 trucks, 28 cars, and one motorcycle—a total of 45 vehicles—were stranded on the icy highway.

15. About eight hundred people attended the eight seminars, which were held at the Civic Center, One Nash Street, in Erie.

16. Originally planned for the 21st of June, the wedding is now the third of July.

17. President Arroyo has reserved Suite 3,201 for the conference that begins in 10 days.

18. Creole Wholesale is located at 2828 West Twenty-second Street in New Orleans.

19. Twenty-three board members voted against the extention of the filing date; three members waived their right to vote.

20. While shopping at the new mall, I spent $250 for a coat, $24.95 for a sweater, $60.00 for shoes, $59.99 for a watch, and 99 cents for socks.

     Name ________________________

*Use the appropriate proofreading symbols to mark errors in the expression of numbers and in spelling. Write **C** after the sentence if it is correct.*

1. Is the Perkins' estate really worth over six million dollars? *[marked: $6]*

2. More than twenty absences will result in the loss of your license. *[marked: (or 20); c]*

3. Last year 15 employees entered the marathon, but only 7 completed it. C

4. One hundred seventy-eight positions were posted by Mrs. Galakatos last month. *[marked: posted 178]*

5. Chase's new store has 16,000 square feet, a 20% increase in floor space.

6. Although Jay's nineth birthday was May 26, his party was held on June 2d.

7. Conference registration is 2 1/2 times what it was 5 years ago.

8. The swimming pool on the fourth floor of the 18-story hotel is 20 feet by 40 feet. C

9. Model No. S-37,289 is described on pages 102 - 104 of the catalog.

10. Carla has accummulated almost thirty thousand frequent flyer points. *[marked: (or 30,000)]*

11. The principal is conscious of the need for fifty 100-page theme books. C

12. More than 1/2 of homeowners have morgages on their residences. *[marked: t]*

13. Please contribute $5.00 toward the party to celebrate the team's 30th win.

14. By 8 o'clock three buses, 14 trucks, 28 cars, and one motorcycle—a total of 48 vehicles—were stranded on the icy highway. *[marked: 3; 1; 6]*

15. About eight hundred people attended the eight seminars, which were held at the Civic Center, One Nash Street, in Erie. *[marked: (or 800)]*

16. Originally planned for the 21st of June, the wedding is now the third of July. *[marked: 3d]*

17. President Arroyo has reserved Suite 3201 for the conference that begins in 10 days.

18. Creole Wholesale is located at 2828 West Twenty-second Street in New Orleans. *[marked: 22d (or 22)]*

19. Twenty-three board members voted against the extention of the filing date; three members waived their right to vote. *[marked: s]*

20. While shopping at the new mall, I spent $250 for a coat, $24.95 for a sweater, $60.00 for shoes, $59.99 for a watch, and 99 cents for socks. *[marked: $.99]*

Name ______________________________

*Use the appropriate proofreading symbols to mark all errors in format. In addition, mark errors in keyboarding, abbreviation, number expression, capitalization, and spelling. Write **C** next to the number if the item is correct.*

1. Harragan Investments
   659 Eighth St.
   Boston, MA 021094100
   Dear Mr. Harragan:

2. April 14, 20--

   Kendall & Associates
   P.O. Box 2439
   Hurst, Tex. 76054-3242

3. Nov. 19, 20--

   Dr. Anthony E. Pritchard, M.D.
   RFD 2, Box 207
   Kalamazoo, MI 49003-3128

   NEW INVESTMENT OFFER

   Dear Dr. Pritchard

4. Sincerely Yours,
   ACME PARTS, INC.

   Miss Hilarie Kreuger
   Senior Vice President

5. Mr. Han Olaski
   All National Insurance corp.
   1409 S. Broadway Boulevard
   Cincinnati, Ohio 45230-2900

   Dear Mr. Han:

   Re: Insured: Boris Metcalf
          Policy No.:   A-42839X
          Date of Loss: 10/24/98

6. Mr. Han Olaski
   Page 2
   3/29/20--

7.   TO: Mailroom Personnel
            FROM: Human Resources
            DATE: January 2, 20--
       SUBJECT: Changes in benefits

8. TO: Mailroom Personnel
   FROM: Human Resources
   Date: January 2, 20--
   SUBJECT: Changes in Benefits

9. Ms. Sue Ellen Sosnowski
   General Counsel
   The New York Times
   229 West 43d Street
   New York NY 10036-0454

   Ladies and Gentlemen:

   CORPORATE SPONSORSHIP

10. Beau O'Neal
    Office of Editor-in-Chief
    The Wall Street Journal
    200 Liberty Avenue
    New York, NY 10081-1217

    Dear Beau O'Neal,

11. Advertising Department
    The Washington Post Corporate Offices
    1150 15th Street, NW
    Washington, DC 20001-9116

    Dear Advertising Department

Match the term to the definitions below by writing the correct letter(s) in the blank provided. More than one letter may be correct.

a. block style, open punctuation
b. block style, mixed punctuation
c. modified block style, open punctuation
d. modified block style, mixed punctuation
e. simplified style

______ 12. Includes a colon after the salutation and a comma after the complementary close.

______ 13. Shows all paragraphs at the left margin.

______ 14. Shows the complementary close at the center.

______ 15. Includes a salutation.

______ 16. Shows everything beginning at the left margin, includes a salutation, but does not include a colon after the salutation.

______ 17. Shows the writer's name keyed in all capital letters.

*Write **T** if the statement is true or **F** is the statement is false.*

______ 18. A report always includes a table of contents.

______ 19. The title page of a report includes five different elements.

______ 20. Title case in a report treats headings with initial capital letters.

______ 21. Reports may be single-spaced or double-spaced.

______ 22. The term *widow/orphan* refers to references that appear on a separate page.

______ 23. A letter or memo transmitting a report is always attached separately from the report and is not bound with it.

______ 24. A list of references used or works cited should be included in an appendix.

______ 25. A bound report has a left margin of 1 inch, and an unbound report has a left margin of 1.5 inches.

______ 26. Page numbers in a report should be centered at the bottom of each page.

Name _______________________

*Use the appropriate proofreading symbols to mark all errors in format. In addition, mark errors in keyboarding, abbreviation, number expression, capitalization, and spelling. Write **C** next to the number if the item is correct.*

1. Harragan Investments
   659 Eighth St.
   Boston, MA 02109-4100
   ~~Dear Mr. Harragan:~~
   Ladies and Gentlemen:

2. April 14, 20--

   Kendall & Associates
   P.O. Box 2439
   Hurst, Tex. 76054-3242
   TX

3. Nov. 19, 20--

   Dr. Anthony E. Pritchard, M.D.
   RFD 2, Box 207
   Kalamazoo, MI 49003-3128

   NEW INVESTMENT OFFER

   Dear Dr. Pritchard

4. Sincerely Yours,
   ACME PARTS, INC.

   Miss Hilarie Kreuger
   Senior Vice President

5. Mr. Han Olaski   (or Corporation)
   All National Insurance corp.
   1409 S. Broadway Boulevard
   Cincinnati, ~~Ohio~~ 45230-2900
   OH

   Dear Mr. Han:

   Re: Insured: Boris Metcalf
         Policy No.:   A-42839X
         Date of Loss: 10/24/98

6. Mr. Han Olaski
   Page 2
   3/29/20--

7.   TO: Mailroom Personnel
        FROM: Human Resources
        DATE: January 2, 20--
     SUBJECT: Changes in benefits

8. TO: Mailroom Personnel
   FROM: Human Resources
   Date: January 2, 20--
   SUBJECT: Changes in Benefits

9. Ms. Sue Ellen Sosnowski
   General Counsel
   The New York Times
   229 West 43d Street
   New York, NY 10036-0454
   Dear Ms. Sosnowski:
   ~~Ladies and Gentlemen:~~

   CORPORATE SPONSORSHIP

10. Beau O'Neal
    Office of Editor-in-Chief
    The Wall Street Journal
    200 Liberty Avenue
    New York, NY 10081-1217

    Dear Beau O'Neal, (or:)

C 11. Advertising Department
       The Washington Post Corporate Offices
       1150 15th Street, NW
       Washington, DC 20001-9116

       Dear Advertising Department

Match the term to the definitions below by writing the correct letter(s) in the blank provided. More than one letter may be correct.

a.   block style, open punctuation
b.   block style, mixed punctuation
c.   modified block style, open punctuation
d.   modified block style, mixed punctuation
e.   simplified style

__B,D__   12. Includes a colon after the salutation and a comma after the complementary close.

__A,B,C,D,E__   13. Shows all paragraphs at the left margin.

__C,D__   14. Shows the complementary close at the center.

__A,B,C,D__   15. Includes a salutation.

__A__   16. Shows everything beginning at the left margin, includes a salutation, but does not include a colon after the salutation.

__E__   17. Shows the writer's name keyed in all capital letters.

*Write **T** if the statement is true or **F** is the statement is false.*

__F__   18. A report always includes a table of contents.

__F__   19. The title page of a report includes five different elements.

__T__   20. Title case in a report treats headings with initial capital letters.

__T__   21. Reports may be single-spaced or double-spaced.

__F__   22. The term *widow/orphan* refers to references that appear on a separate page.

__F__   23. A letter or memo transmitting a report is always attached separately from the report and is not bound with it.

__F__   24. A list of references used or works cited should be included in an appendix.

__F__   25. A bound report has a left margin of 1 inch, and an unbound report has a left margin of 1.5 inches.

__F__   26. Page numbers in a report should be centered at the bottom of each page.

Name ___________________________

*Use the appropriate proofreading symbols to mark all errors in sentence structure. Look for subject-verb agreement, sentence faults, and spelling errors. If necessary, revise the verb to make the subject and verb agree. Write **C** after the sentence if it is correct.*

1. The number of excellent textbooks are making it difficult to reach a unanimus decision.
2. Although Sue can supply some facts on the subject. Takeo can give the best explaination.
3. Each man, woman, and child need to be accomodated in the housing arrangements.
4. Both Cassie and Nick are applying for the academic scholarship.
5. Neither the correspondence nor the filing have been completed.
6. Every one of the letters has to be signed by the personnel director.
7. There are thank-you cards to be written and phone calls to be returned.
8. The restaraunt's chef, as well as the servers, volunteer every Monday at the shelter.
9. Many a sales representative and customer service representative are enrolled in our class.
10. Although most of the library was damaged, a number of books was saved.
11. A small quantity of raw lumber for the research department are being ordered today.
12. Over half of the time allowed for questions were lost because of the fire drill.
13. Anyone of us can train you to write formulas in a spreadsheet, Mika is the best trainer.
14. Has the word processing standards been published in the bulletin?
15. Across the street Noah and Trudy was shouting at each another Trudy was also crying.
16. One of the reasons for the decline in sales are lack of good advertising.
17. The administrative assistant for those two departments are very busy during the holidays.
18. The presenter noticed the audience were in turmoil over the change in schedule.
19. Most of the proposals appear to contain some truth and some exageration.
20. Our president and chairman of the board, Monica J. Sampras, say the company have to make consessions in the market to stay competitive.

Name ___________________________

*Use the appropriate proofreading symbols to mark all errors in sentence structure. Look for subject-verb agreement, sentence faults, and spelling errors. If necessary, revise the verb to make the subject and verb agree. Write **C** after the sentence if it is correct.*

1. The number of excellent textbooks *is* making it difficult to reach a unanimous decision.

2. Although Sue can supply some facts on the subject, Takeo can give the best explaination.

3. Each man, woman, and child need to be accomodated in the housing arrangements.

4. Both Cassie and Nick are applying for the academic scholarship. C

5. Neither the correspondence nor the filing *has* been completed.

6. Every one of the letters has to be signed by the personnel director. C

7. There are thank-you cards to be written and phone calls to be returned. C

8. The restaraunt's chef, as well as the servers, volunteer every Monday at the shelter.

9. Many a sales representative and customer service representative *is* enrolled in our class.

10. Although most of the library was damaged, a number of books *were* saved.

11. A small quantity of raw lumber for the research department *is* being ordered today.

12. Over half of the time allowed for questions *was* lost because of the fire drill.

13. Anyone of us can train you to write formulas in a spreadsheet, Mika is the best trainer.

14. *Have* Has the word processing standards been published in the bulletin?

15. Across the street Noah and Trudy *were* shouting at each another, Trudy was also crying.

16. One of the reasons for the decline in sales *is* lack of good advertising.

17. The administrative assistant for those two departments *is* very busy during the holidays.

18. The presenter noticed the audience *was* in turmoil over the change in schedule.

19. Most of the proposals appear to contain some truth and some exaggeration.

20. Our president and chairman of the board, Monica J. Sampras, says the company *has* to make concessions in the market to stay competitive.

Name _______________________

*Use the appropriate proofreading symbols to mark all errors in pronoun selection and spelling. Also, edit words that should reflect gender-neutral language. Write **C** after the sentence if it is correct.*

1. Whom did you ask to help Rajesh and I?

2. Just between you and I, she is being transferred next month.

3. The U.S. Supreme Court handed down it's decision yesterday.

4. If you were she, would you take possession of the morgage at this time?

5. If Irene comes, Charlie is going to ask she to present the award.

6. The group from the women's choir appears to have her paperwork in order.

7. Judd and Ernesto are helping Derek and she with the bulk mailing job.

8. An airline pilot will usually give a weather update to his passengers.

9. Are you and him going to give Justin and her a farewell party?

10. Were you surprised by them resigning so early in the year?

11. Only a few employees volunteered his or her time on the clean-up crew.

12. Renee often receives both praise and critisicm for her creative work.

13. Who did you say is responsable for putting together a commitee?

14. You achieving the highest sales goal came as no surprise to the other salesmen.

15. The company president honored we employees for our community service.

16. A good English teacher will teach her students the rule about each pronoun agreeing with their antecedent.

17. No one but myself will know the outcome of the vote until it's announced tonight.

18. It could have been him who delivered the message to me earlier in the day.

19. Their are plans in the making for permanantly decreasing the speed limit.

20. Her marketing plan is highly regarded and is more widely reconized than our's.

*Use the appropriate proofreading symbols to mark all errors in pronoun selection and spelling. Also, edit words that should reflect gender-neutral language. Write **C** after the sentence if it is correct.*

1. Whom did you ask to help Rajesh and ~~I~~ [me]?

2. Just between you and ~~I~~ [me], she is being transferred next month.

3. The U.S. Supreme Court handed down it~~'~~s decision yesterday.

4. If you were she, would you take possession of the mor[t]gage at this time?

5. If Irene comes, Charlie is going to ask ~~she~~ [her] to present the award.

6. The group from the women's choir appears to have ~~her~~ [its] paperwork in order.

7. Judd and Ernesto are helping Derek and ~~she~~ [her] with the bulk mailing job.

8. An airline pilot will usually give a weather update to ~~his~~ [the (or his or her)] passengers.

9. Are you and ~~him~~ [he] going to give Justin and her a farewell party?

10. Were you surprised by ~~them~~ [their] resigning so early in the year?

11. Only a few employees volunteered ~~his or her~~ [their] time on the clean-up crew.

12. Renee often receives both praise and criti[c]i[s]m for her creative work.

13. Who did you say is respons[i]ble for putting together a commit[t]ee?

14. You[r] achieving the highest sales goal came as no surprise to the other sales~~men~~ [people]. (or sales representatives or staff)

15. The company president honored ~~we~~ [us] employees for our community service.

16. A good English teacher will teach ~~her~~ [the (or his or her)] students the rule about each pronoun agreeing with ~~their~~ [its] antecedent.

17. No one but ~~myself~~ [me] will know the outcome of the vote until it's announced tonight.

18. It could have been ~~him~~ [he] who delivered the message to me earlier in the day.

19. ~~Their~~ [There] are plans in the making for perman[e]ntly decreasing the speed limit.

20. Her marketing plan is highly regarded and is more widely reco[g]nized than our~~'~~s.

                     Name ___________________________

*Use the appropriate proofreading symbols to mark all errors in word selection and spelling. Write **C** after the sentence if it is correct.*

1. I ensure any unique or valueable objects in case I loose them.

2. We felt badly about the negative reaction to the proposed zoning changes.

3. Receiving a genuine complement is always appreciated.

4. Will Shipley was appointed to serve as counsel for the defendant.

5. I noticed that people brought less salads to this month's potluck.

6. No matter how good we proofread these address lists, we seem to miss something.

7. Irregardless of what we thought, Chet past his driving exam with a perfect score.

8. Heather recommends that we make the pay increases retroactive from January 1.

9. It looks like the supervisors are already to discuss the annual evaluations.

10. Be sure to mention the Internet sites you found during your research.

11. My expereince is that one must be careful about taking other people's advise.

12. The high temperature in the room had a negative effect on the workers.

13. Riding a stationary bicycle is a good every day exercise.

14. I will bring my new laptop tomorrow, and you can bring it home for a few days.

15. Increased fuel prices preceeded the decline in sales of new automobiles.

16. My neighbor, which is a master gardener, will show us how to prune fruit trees.

17. After the crew lays the new carpet, I want you to lay on it to see how it feels.

18. Wini Chavez, principal of the high school, gave the all together humorous address at the Chamber of Commerce banquet.

19. He ommitted to many names from the list of prospective customers.

20. Frannie implied she would be interested in attending the sort a seminar that teaches the pyschology of how to deal with conflict in the workplace.

*Use the appropriate proofreading symbols to mark all errors in word selection and spelling. Write **C** after the sentence if it is correct.*

1. I ensure any unique or valuable objects in case I loose them.

2. We felt badly about the negative reaction to the proposed zoning changes.

3. Receiving a genuine complement is always appreciated.

4. Will Shipley was appointed to serve as counsel for the defendant. *C*

5. I noticed that people brought ~~less~~ *fewer* salads to this month's potluck.

6. No matter how ~~good~~ *well* we proofread these address lists, we seem to miss something.

7. ~~I~~rregardless of what we thought, Chet ~~past~~ *passed* his driving exam with a perfect score.

8. Heather recommends that we make the pay increases retroactive ~~from~~ *to* January 1.

9. It looks ~~like~~ *as if* the supervisors are ~~already~~ *all ready* to discuss the annual evaluations.

10. Be sure to mention the Internet sites you found during your research. *C*

11. My experience is that one must be careful about taking other people's advise.

12. The high temperature in the room had a negative effect on the workers. *C*

13. Riding a stationary bicycle is a good every day exercise.

14. I will bring my new laptop tomorrow, and you can ~~bring~~ *take* it home for a few days.

15. Increased fuel prices preceeded the decline in sales of new automobiles.

16. My neighbor, ~~which~~ *who* is a master gardener, will show us how to prune fruit trees.

17. After the crew lays the new carpet, I want you to ~~lay~~ *lie* on it to see how it feels.

18. Wini Chavez, principal of the high school, gave the all together humorous address at the Chamber of Commerce banquet.

19. He ommitted to many names from the list of prospective customers.

20. Frannie implied she would be interested in attending the sort *of* a seminar that teaches the psychology of how to deal with conflict in the workplace.

*Use the appropriate proofreading symbols to mark all punctuation and spelling errors. Write **C** after the sentence if it is correct.*

1. Philomene notes that her job is highly stressful, but says that having a significant degree of freedom is important to her.

2. Tina will cook and Joy will wash dishes. Both girls have enthusiastic diligent attitudes toward work.

3. The transition from typing to word processing was fairly easy, and the transition from word processing to desktop publishing was also relatively easy.

4. Learning more about working with computers, gave me the opportunity to take initiative, to learn new skills and to increase my contribution to the company.

5. In Row 10, 12 seats are available for the Saturday, December 10 dress rehearsal.

6. I have the priviledge of reporting that our industrious knowledgeable representatives have increased our sales volume by 20 percent.

7. Every computer-generated slide show should include a title slide, a central theme and a format that is easy to read. By following an outline and simple instructions even amatures can create an attractive slide show.

8. We moved to Nashville, Tennessee in June 1990 so that we could spend more of our liesure time in the Smokies.

9. Because he has been transfered to Denver Dr. Santoyo must sell his house.

10. This report includes your account balance at the beginning of our fiscal quarter, your savings during the quarter and our investment results.

11. His iteneray includes a lecture in Des Moines, Iowa on June 18, and a second lecture in Grand Rapids, Michigan on June 22.

12. The lawyer asked, "Did Everett fulfil his obligations on time?"

13. Cheng bought an oak dresser, an antique chair, a wool rug and a hat at the auction

14. Will you serve as the laision between the buyer and the seller.

15. Roscoe is pleased with the development of the subdivision, and is planning to begin selling lots at the home show that opens Saturday, May 2 at 10 a.m..

*Use the appropriate proofreading symbols to mark all punctuation and spelling errors. Write **C** after the sentence if it is correct.*

1. Philomene notes that her job is highly stressful but says that having a significant degree of freedom is important to her.

2. Tina will cook and Joy will wash dishes. Both girls have enthusiastic diligent attitudes toward work.

3. The transition from typing to word processing was fairly easy, and the transition from word processing to desktop publishing was also relatively easy. C

4. Learning more about working with computers gave me the opportunity to take initiative, to learn new skills and to increase my contribution to the company.

5. In Row 10, 12 seats are available for the Saturday, December 10 dress rehearsal.

6. I have the priviledge of reporting that our industrious knowledgeable representatives have increased our sales volume by 20 percent.

7. Every computer-generated slide show should include a title slide, a central theme and a format that is easy to read. By following an outline and simple instructions even amatures can create an attractive slide show.

8. We moved to Nashville, Tennessee in June 1990 so that we could spend more of our liesure time in the Smokies.

9. Because he has been transfered to Denver Dr. Santoyo must sell his house.

10. This report includes your account balance at the beginning of our fiscal quarter, your savings during the quarter and our investment results.

11. His itineray includes a lecture in Des Moines, Iowa on June 18 and a second lecture in Grand Rapids, Michigan on June 22.

12. The lawyer asked, "Did Everett fulfil his obligations on time?"

13. Cheng bought an oak dresser, an antique chair, a wool rug and a hat at the auction

14. Will you serve as the laison between the buyer and the seller?

15. Roscoe is pleased with the development of the subdivision and is planning to begin selling lots at the home show that opens Saturday, May 2 at 10 a.m.

        Name ___________________________________

*Use the appropriate proofreading symbols to mark all punctuation and spelling errors. Write **C** after the sentence if it is correct.*

1. Home-automation systems—known as "smart house" systems may become commonplace within a few years.

2. His hectic calendar included: an 11 a.m. meeting to review a product presentation; a 2:00 p.m. phone call with a new manager; and a 4 p.m. quarterly meeting with the marketing director.

3. Its anyone's guess where Herb's and Daisy's dog has gone.

4. An office design is often based on preconceived ideas of how space should be used, but buildings, furnishings, and equipment are merely tools.

5. As she graciously closed her address, Dr. Saleh said, "It has been a pleasure to be here today. Once again, thank you for inviting me. I would like to close with a quote from my mentor who says, Success in life is a matter of perseverance."

6. Only 12 percent said they would marry for money alone; undoubtedly, this is a minority opinion.

7. The bankrupcy judge ruled that it is permissable for the CPA, Certified Public Accountant, to complete her analysis of the debtor's proposal.

8. I always read D. L. Willman's column entitled Money Matters in The Evening Post.

9. Morton admitted: "I am proud of my son-in-laws' (Lou Johanson) achievments.

10. Miss Starn posed an interesting question—Should our retirement plan parrallel the one First Bank has proposed?

11. Some suggestions for caring for your skin are: (a) quit smoking, (b) drink sufficient water, c) exercise regularly, and d) use a moisturizer every day.

12. Send notices to Mr. Jason Rose, PLS, at Moffatt Thomas, Mrs. Jada Zarle, PLS, at Hall Farley, and Ms. Gloria Ayala, ALS, at Hawley Troxell.

13. Call me by 10:15 a.m., I need your answer before I leave at 11:00 a.m.

14. Hard work, initiative, and luck: success requires these three ingredients.

15. Insurance forms a strong foundation for most financial plans, therefore, its wise to get help in determining how much you need.

Use the appropriate proofreading symbols to mark all punctuation and spelling errors. Write **C** *after the sentence if it is correct.*

1. Home-automation systems—known as "smart house" systems may become commonplace within a few years.

2. His hectic calendar included an 11 a.m. meeting to review a product presentation, a 2:00 p.m. phone call with a new manager, and a 4 p.m. quarterly meeting with the marketing director.

3. Its anyone's guess where Herb's and Daisy's dog has gone.

4. An office design is often based on preconceived ideas of how space should be used, but buildings, furnishings, and equipment are merely tools.

5. As she graciously closed her address, Dr. Saleh said, "It has been a pleasure to be here today. Once again, thank you for inviting me. I would like to close with a quote from my mentor who says, 'Success in life is a matter of perseverance.'"

6. Only 12 percent said they would marry for money alone; undoubtedly, this is a minority opinion. C

7. The bankrupcy judge ruled that it is permissable for the CPA (Certified Public Accountant) to complete her analysis of the debtor's proposal.

8. I always read D. L. Willman's column entitled Money Matters in The Evening Post.

9. Morton admitted, "I am proud of my son-in-law's (Lou Johanson) achievments."

10. Miss Starn posed an interesting question—Should our retirement plan parallel the one First Bank has proposed?

11. Some suggestions for caring for your skin are (a) quit smoking, (b) drink sufficient water, (c) exercise regularly, and (d) use a moisturizer every day.

12. Send notices to Mr. Jason Rose, PLS, at Moffatt Thomas, Mrs. Jada Zarle, PLS, at Hall Farley, and Ms. Gloria Ayala, ALS, at Hawley Troxell.

13. Call me by 10:15 a.m. I need your answer before I leave at 11:00 a.m.

14. Hard work, initiative, and luck success requires these three ingredients.

15. Insurance forms a strong foundation for most financial plans, therefore, its wise to get help in determining how much you need.

    Name ___________________________________

*Use the appropriate proofreading symbols to mark all capitalization and spelling errors. Write **C** after the sentence if it is correct.*

1. Our company is moving its headquarters to the east coast.

2. When the President of the United States hosted the Pope last summer, the first lady used the newly designed white house China.

3. Arlene's puppy is a Boston Terrier. Is that a minature breed?

4. Did you know that my Ford Automobile has a Sony Tape Player?

5. Let's emphasize one point: Perseverence of a goal pays off in most cases.

6. When Mayor-Elect Shaughnessy appeared at the Azalea festival, she expressed gratitude for the warm hospitality shown to her.

7. Bert Fischler, Ph.D., received his B.F.A. degree from Campbell college; he now works as an Engineer at General Electric's Cincinnati Plant.

8. Look for the map in Volume 4, Appendix C, Page 361, of the *Columbia Review.*

9. Wayne Mackey, Chief Executive Officer, Monroe Paints, has announced plans for expansion of the company's Southern chain stores.

10. Both the Supervisor and the General Manager apologized to the workers for not discussing the change in working hours with them.

11. Graham has been employed to work in our engineering department, which is located in the Yim building on the North end of the office complex.

12. Ms. Holden, who has a Master's Degree in music, will teach Music Theory 311 at the university.

13. Forrey Travel agency sent an aknowledgement to me regarding my reservations on Delta flight 274, which departs from Gate 15 at 6:18 P.M.

14. You should know how to use the following software programs: Word Processing, Spreadsheet, and Database.

15. A fastenating documentary entitled "Life on ice: Antarctica and Mars" received a good review from *The Rockville Times.*

*Use the appropriate proofreading symbols to mark all capitalization and spelling errors. Write **C** after the sentence if it is correct.*

1. Our company is moving its headquarters to the east coast.

2. When the President of the United States hosted the Pope last summer, the first lady used the newly designed white house China.

3. Arlene's puppy is a Boston Terrier. Is that a miniature breed?

4. Did you know that my Ford Automobile has a Sony Tape Player?

5. Let's emphasize one point: Perseverance of a goal pays off in most cases.

6. When Mayor-Elect Shaughnessy appeared at the Azalea festival, she expressed gratitude for the warm hospitality shown to her.

7. Bert Fischler, Ph.D., received his B.F.A. degree from Campbell college; he now works as an Engineer at General Electric's Cincinnati Plant.

8. Look for the map in Volume 4, Appendix C, Page 361, of the *Columbia Review*.

9. Wayne Mackey, Chief Executive Officer, Monroe Paints, has announced plans for expansion of the company's Southern chain stores.

10. Both the Supervisor and the General Manager apologized to the workers for not discussing the change in working hours with them.

11. Graham has been employed to work in our engineering department, which is located in the Yim building on the North end of the office complex.

12. Ms. Holden, who has a Master's Degree in music, will teach Music Theory 311 at the university.

13. Forrey Travel agency sent an aknowledgement to me regarding my reservations on Delta flight 274, which departs from Gate 15 at 6:18 P.M.

14. You should know how to use the following software programs: Word Processing, Spreadsheet, and Database.

15. A fascinating documentary entitled "Life on ice: Antarctica and Mars" received a good review from *The Rockville Times*.

Use the appropriate proofreading symbols to mark all errors, concentrating on content. Assume that information is correct the first time it appears. The letter format is modified block.

Tri-States Insurance Company   1701 Landis Street   Phoenix, AZ 85027-6394

1   September 4, 20--

2   Mr. R. A Vaughan
3   Personnel Director
4   McDavid Associates, Inc.
5   3747 Jefferson Street
6   Sausalito, CA 94965-1047

7   Dear Mrs. Vaughan:

8   Thank you for letting our agent, Ms. Melinda Lassiter, present our health insurance
9   plans to you on September 12.

10   Since that time, however, we have impleminted a new health insurance plan especially
11   for members of the National Society for Electrical Engineers (NSEE). If your company is
12   a member, then you employees are eligible for this insurance. Call Ms. Lasiter for more
13   information about this special plan for N.S.E.E. members.

14   You probably no, Mr. Vaughn, that Tri-State Insurance Company is independantly
15   owned. We offer a variety of insurance coverage, and a staff of agents whose effeciency
16   and productivity are unequaled. They will happy to help you with your company's
17   insurance needs.

18   An up-to-date brochure about our many programs is enclosed. Please look it over,
19   Mr. Vaughan, to determine the best program for McDavis Associates Inc. If you need
20   more information, please contact Mrs. Lassiter or me at 555-0125.

21   Sincerely,

22   Eli E. Hargett
23   Marketing Manager

24   jl

Name ________________________

Use the appropriate proofreading symbols to mark all errors, concentrating on content. Assume that information is correct the first time it appears. The letter format is modified block.

Tri-States Insurance Company   1701 Landis Street   Phoenix, AZ 85027-6394

1   September 4 20--

2   Mr. R. A. Vaughan
3   Personnel Director
4   McDavid Associates, Inc.
5   3747 Jefferson Street
6   Sausalito, CA 94965-1047

7   Dear Mrs. Vaughan:

8   Thank you for letting our agent, Ms. Melinda Lassiter, present our health insurance
9   plans to you on September 12.

10   Since that time, however, we have impleminted a new health insurance plan especially
11   for members of the National Society for Electrical Engineers (NSEE). If your company is
12   a member, then you employees are eligible for this insurance. Call Ms. Lasiter for more
13   information about this special plan for NSEE members.

14   You probably no, Mr. Vaughn, that Tri-State Insurance Company is independantly
15   owned. We offer a variety of insurance coverage, and a staff of agents whose effeciency
16   and productivity are unequaled. They will happy to help you with your company's
17   insurance needs.

18   An up-to-date brochure about our many programs is enclosed. Please look it over,
19   Mr. Vaughan, to determine the best program for McDavis Associates Inc. If you need
20   more information, please contact Mrs. Lassiter or me at 555-0125.

21   Sincerely,

22   Eli E. Hargett
23   Marketing Manager

24   jl
       Enclosure

                                    Name ________________________

Use the appropriate proofreading symbol to mark all errors, concentrating on conciseness. Change all passive voice to active voice. Assume the format is correct.

1   WOMEN AND STRESS

2   Stress is an undeniable part of everyday life. Fortunately, not all stress is bad.

3   Good stress can help you take the bull by the horns and review that presentation once

4   more until such time as you have got it right. When a situation induces chronic anxiety

5   or hostility, you are dealing with bad stress.

6   How we respond to any potentially stressful situation—called a stressor—is

7   influenced by two factors: our general approach to life and the number of stressors we

8   have at once. Irregardless of our mental outlook, research at this point in time shows that

9   our approach to stress can change and bad stressors can be converted into good ones.

10   First, the causes of stress need to be identified. Research has revealed the

11   following common sources of stress affecting women: worry about the future, too much

12   to do, not enough time, and too much responsibility.

13   The honest truth is that you can deal with stress. Consider these three ways to

14   bite the bullet and deal with stress: Change the situation, change the response, or find

15   ways to deflect the tension. In the event that the problem can be solved, it should be

16   solved. For example, if you do not get along with a person in managment, then the

17   bottom line is you have to decide whether to stay in the job or leave. If leaving the job is

18   unrealistic, then you must turn over a new leaf and your response to this person must

19   change.

20   As a final thought, remember that exercise, relaxation techniques, and social

21   interaction help to reduce stress. Many women suffering from stress have benefitted

22   from including these activities in their lives; you might benefit from including them in

23   yours.

Use the appropriate proofreading symbol to mark all errors, concentrating on conciseness. Change all passive voice to active voice. Assume the format is correct.

1 WOMEN AND STRESS

2 Stress is an undeniable part of everyday life. Fortunately, not all stress is bad.

3 Good stress can help you take ~~the bull by the horns~~ and review that presentation once
   control

4 more until ~~such time as~~ you have ~~got~~ it right. When a situation induces chronic anxiety

5 or hostility, you are dealing with bad stress.

6 How we respond to any potentially stressful situation—called a stressor—is

7 influenced by two factors: our general approach to life and the number of stressors we

8 have at once. ~~Irregardless~~ of our mental outlook, research ~~at this point in time~~ shows that
         Regardless   *current*

9 our approach to stress can change and bad stressors ~~can be converted~~ into good ones.
                    we   *convert*

10 First, the causes of stress ~~need to be identified~~. Research has revealed the
    identify

11 following common sources of stress affecting women: worry about the future, too much

12 to do, not enough time, and too much responsibility.

13 The ~~honest~~ truth is that you can deal with stress. Consider these three ways to

14 ~~bite the bullet and~~ deal with stress: Change the situation, change the response, or find
                                            If

15 ways to deflect the tension. ~~In the event that~~ the problem can be solved, it should be

16 solved. For example, if you do not get along with a person in managment, then ~~the~~
                                                                      e

17 ~~bottom line is~~ you have to decide whether to stay in the job or leave. If leaving the job is

18 unrealistic, then you must ~~turn over a new leaf and~~ your response to this person ~~must~~
                               change

19 ~~change.~~
       Finally

20 ~~As a final thought~~, remember that exercise, relaxation techniques, and social

21 interaction help to reduce stress. Many women suffering from stress have benefitted

22 from including these activities in their lives; you might benefit from including them in

23 yours.

Name ______________________________

Use the appropriate proofreading symbols to mark all errors, concentrating on clarity. The letter format is block.

1   April 28, 20--

2   Mr. Mario Buzzelli

3   2864 Valencia Avenue

4   San Diego, CA 92109-0864

5   Dear Mr. Buzzelli:

6   Welcome to Pacific National Bank! We are delighted to have you as a customer.

7   Our bank is a throughly comprehensive financial institution. Our services encompass checking

8   and savings accounts, certificates of deposit, safe-deposit boxes, automatic tellers, and personal

9   bankers. From talking with customers, the belief is that our services are what people need. We

10   think you, too, will find it advantageous to do business with a full-service bank.

11   You will find our service charge on checking accounts to be not only quite low but also very

12   competitive with rates found in other banks. However, we are cognizant of the inconvenience of

13   a service charge. Therefore, we initiated development of a plan that eliminates checking account

14   charges. By opening and maintaining a savings account with a balance of at least $25, no service

15   charge will be made on your checking account.

16   We realize your work schedule is demanding and how valuable your time is. That is why we

17   have assigned Claire Vizcarra as your personal banker. You can obtain valuable advice from Ms.

18   Vizcarra. She also has the authority to approve your personal loans. We think you will find her

19   to be conscienteous, courteus, and you will enjoy working with her.

20   If you have questions about our free checking plan or any of the other services offered at Pacific

21   National Bank, please contact your personal banker, Ms. Vizcarra.

22   Sincerely,

23   Zachary P. Fisher

24   Vice President

25   th

Name ___________________________

Use the appropriate proofreading symbols to mark all errors, concentrating on clarity. The letter format is block.

1   April 28, 20--

2   Mr. Mario Buzzelli

3   2864 Valencia Avenue

4   San Diego, CA 92109-0864

5   Dear Mr. Buzzelli:

6   Welcome to Pacific National Bank! We are delighted to have you as a customer.

7   Our bank is a throughly comprehensive financial institution. Our services encompass [include] checking

8   and savings accounts, certificates of deposit, safe-deposit boxes, automatic tellers, and personal

9   bankers. From talking with customers, the belief is [we believe] that our services are what people need. We

10   think you, too, will find it advantageous to do business with a full-service bank.

11   You will find our service charge on checking accounts to be not only quite low but also very

12   competitive with rates found in other banks. However, we are cognizant of [realize] the inconvenience of

13   a service charge. Therefore, we initiated development of [developed] a plan that eliminates checking account

14   charges. By opening and maintaining a savings account with a balance of at least $25, [you will incur] no service

15   charge will be made on your checking account.

16   We realize your work schedule is demanding and how valuable your time is. That is why we

17   have assigned Claire Vizcarra as your personal banker. You can obtain [can give you] valuable advice from Ms.

18   Vizcarra. She also has the authority to approve your personal loans. We think you will find her

19   to be conscientious, courteous, and you will enjoy working with her. [a pleasure to work with.]

20   If you have questions about our free checking plan or any of the other services offered at Pacific

21   National Bank, please contact your personal banker, Ms. Vizcarra.

22   Sincerely,

23   Zachary P. Fisher

24   Vice President

25   th

                    Name ___________________________

Proofread each of the following sentences for mechanical errors (spelling, abbreviation, word division, number expression, grammar, punctuation, capitalization), content errors, conciseness, and clarity. Use the appropriate proofreading symbols to indicate corrections. Sentences often contain more than one error. If a sentence is correct, write C after it.

1. It was he who called.

2. Send letters to whomever is on the list.

3. No one can spell as well as her.

4. Urbana, Wooten, and Gaylord, Inc., will move their office to Vermont.

5. One criterion for selecting the textbook is cost.

6. Our historian and reporter, Tyrone Abel, has done a good job.

7. Here is the book and tape that you requested.

8. A number of children is enrolled in the Summer reading program.

9. Everyone has his or her own problems.

10. Three honor students in art Kim, Pablo, and Ali were recognized at the awards ceremony.

11. Many people drop the *s* from Dr. Hastings' name.

12. An error tolerance of 0.05 percent is permissable.

13. Yes, the team has all ready made their decision.

14. Will you please purchase 12 16-ounce tumblers?

15. Fantastic! We won the $10 million lottery!

16. Delta Flight 210 leaves from gate 7 at 8 a.m. on October 14.

17. S. America sells a lot of coffee to the United States.

18. To make this jacket you will need 3 yards of 54-inch-wide material.

19. Jeanne Brillhart was transferred to the Loan department.

20. About two thousand people attended the Raleigh Summer Festival on July 29th.

21. More than three-fourths of the stockholders voted on the 13 proposed changes.

22. Lynn Hengle, M.D., has opened an office in the Brody Building which is located at 5410 West Eighth Street, Topeka, Kansas.

23. Beau is 6 feet 6 inches tall, and he has difficulty getting into his sports car.

24. The Goodwill Games, which were held in Seattle were telecast by WTBS-TV.

25. Laurie paid $2.45 for the card and $6.25 for the booklet, making the total $8.60.

Clarion Fire Systems

1266 East Windsor Road
Pontiac, MI 48054-1266

June 10, 20--

Mr. Antoine Monsanto
General Manager
Conseco Garage Doors, Inc.
14007 Mission Way
Phoenix, AZ 85018-1290

Gentlemen:

Thank you for your recent inquiry about our fire alarm protection service. The purpose of this letter is to inform you that we have many options from which to choose and we would be pleased to discuss your needs and which system would be the best one for your company.

Our Regional Distributor, Preston Cagle of Red Rock Arizona has been given your name and letter of inquiry. You will be contacted soon by Mr. Cagle to arrange a meeting at your convenience. He will need to tour your facilities before he can make a recommendation regarding the fire alarm protection service your company need. After our initial recommendation has been made; we will prepare a final report that includes a bid.

Thank you again for contacting Clarion Fire Systems. We are anxious to help you protect Conceso Garage Doors.

Sincerely yours,
Clarion Fire Systems

Yoko Yamaguchi
Distribution Manager

c Preston Cagle

*Proofread each of the following sentences for mechanical errors (spelling, abbreviation, word division, number expression, grammar, punctuation, capitalization), content errors, conciseness, and clarity. Use the appropriate proofreading symbols to indicate corrections. Sentences often contain more than one error. If a sentence is correct, write **C** after it.*

1. It was he who called. *C*

2. Send letters to whomever is on the list.

3. No one can spell as well as her. [she]

4. Urbana, Wooten, and Gaylord, Inc., will move their [its] office to Vermont.

5. One criterion for selecting the textbook is cost. *C*

6. Our historian and reporter, Tyrone Abel, has done a good job. *C*

7. Here is [are] the book and tape that you requested.

8. A number of children is [are] enrolled in the Summer reading program.

9. Everyone has his or her own problems. *C*

10. Three honor students in art Kim, Pablo, and Ali were recognized at the awards ceremony.

11. Many people drop the *s* from Dr. Hastings' name. *C*

12. An error tolerance of 0.05 percent is permissable. [i — permissible]

13. Yes, the team has already made their [its] decision.

14. Will you please purchase 12 [twelve] 16-ounce tumblers?

15. Fantastic! We won the $10 million lottery! *C*

16. Delta Flight 210 leaves from gate 7 at 8 a.m. on October 14.

17. S. America sells a lot of coffee to the United States.

18. To make this jacket you will need 3 yards of 54-inch-wide material.

19. Jeanne Brillhart was transferred to the Loan department.

20. About two thousand people attended the Raleigh Summer Festival on July 29th.

21. More than three-fourths of the stockholders voted on the 13 proposed changes. *C*

22. Lynn Hengle, M.D., has opened an office in the Brody Building which is located at 5410 West Eighth Street, Topeka, Kansas.

23. Beau is 6 feet 6 inches tall, and he has difficulty getting into his sports car. *C*

24. The Goodwill Games, which were held in Seattle were telecast by WTBS-TV.

25. Laurie paid $2.45 for the card and $6.25 for the booklet, making the total $8.60. [7]

Proofread the following letter for mechanical and content errors. Change passive voice to active voice. The letter should be formatted in modified block style with mixed punctuation. Use the appropriate proofreading symbols to indicate changes.

Clarion Fire Systems

1266 East Windsor Road
Pontiac, MI 48054-1266

June 10, 20--

Mr. Antoine Monsanto
General Manager
Conseco Garage Doors, Inc.
14007 Mission Way
Phoenix, AZ 85018-1290

Dear Mr. Monsanto
~~Gentlemen~~:

Thank you for your recent inquiry about our fire alarm protection service. ~~The purpose of this letter is to inform you that~~ we have many options from which to choose and we would be pleased to discuss your needs and which system would be the best one for your company.

We forwarded your letter of inquiry to
Our Regional Distributor, Preston Cagle of Red Rock, Arizona ~~has been given your name and letter of inquiry. You will be contacted soon by~~ Mr. Cagle will call you within a week to arrange a meeting at your convenience. He will need to tour your facilities before he can ~~make a~~ recommend ~~ation regarding~~ the fire alarm protection service your company needs. After we make our initial recommendation ~~has been made,~~ we will prepare a final report that includes a bid.

Thank you again for contacting Clarion Fire Systems. We are ~~anxious~~ eager to help you protect Conseco Garage Doors.

DS
Sincerely yours,
Clarion Fire Systems

Yoko Yamaguchi
Distribution Manager

c Preston Cagle